THE GLEAMING MAN

text by
Jeremy Fernando

alongside paintings by
Ruben Pang

with a triptych of poems by
Lim Lee Ching

Delere Press

This paperback edition first published in 2018
by Delere Press LLP

Block 370G Alexandra Road
#09-09 Singapore 159960
www.delerepress.com

Delere Press LLP reg no. T11LL1061K

Designed by Sarah and Schooling

© text by Jeremy Fernando, 2018
© paintings by Ruben Pang, 2018
© poems by Lim Lee Ching, 2018
© *Impromptu* by Peter Krakauer, 1971, reproduced with permission

All Rights Reserved

ISBN: 978-981-11-8287-7

for our dear friend, Adam Staley Groves
for our dear friend, Adam Staley Groves

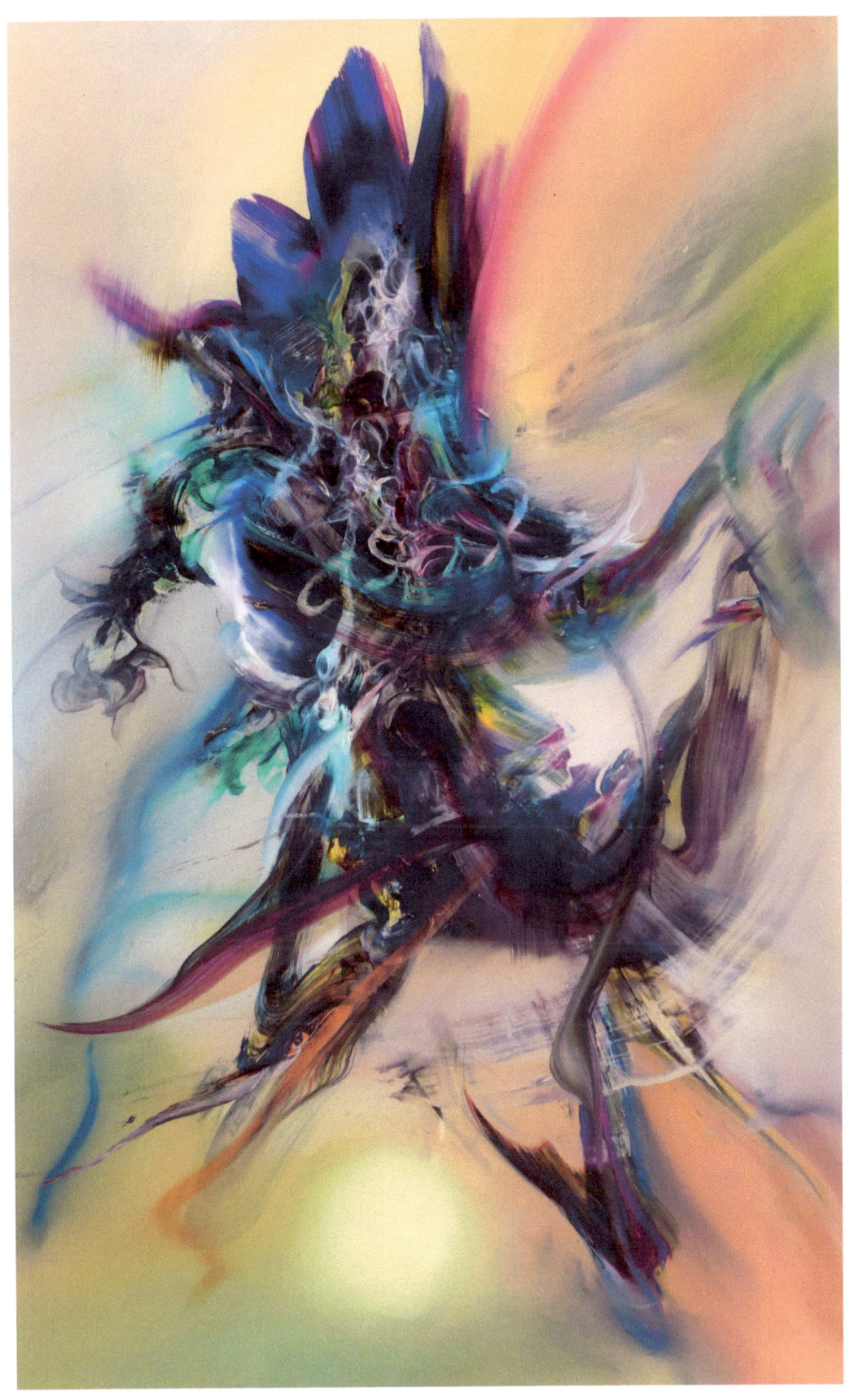

Original Gore

Passacaglia 1 — Gleaming Man

Squared corners, four to the scaffold
Taut board set against the warpings
Of a world blazing in coldness
And sparkles of deep fragile eagerness

Despair is not a medium
It grips the writhing struggles of a
Cloudward gutterance to release
The soft forms of instinctive nurturance

Acclaiming vitality by design
This walled hymn is surface and skin
Breached only by the tiding spots of joy
A token of demand even an exchange[1]

Between seeing and making thoughtful
Role reversals of dulcet memories
This flash of probable promise
Emptying into the eye of a beholder

Lim Lee Ching

---

[1] cf: Robert Browning

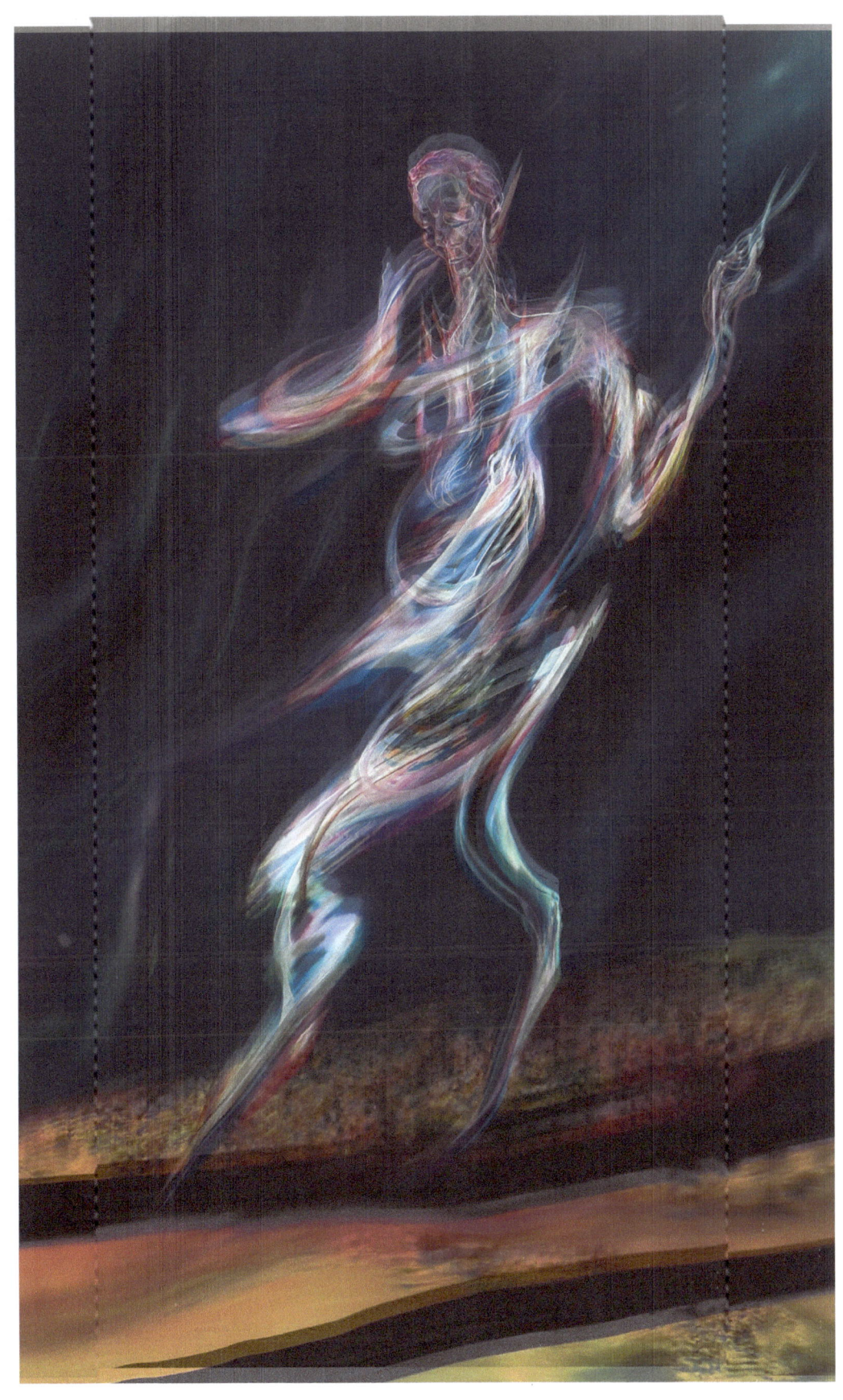

My body likes sin cold
My body likes sin cold

For, angels don't seem to have
any hands ...

So, so you think you can tell
Heaven from hell
Blue skies from pain
Can you tell a green field
From a cold steel rail?
A smile from a veil?
Do you think you can tell?

— David Gilmour & Roger Waters

Blue skies make us sadder than grey skies because they offer us hopes which we do not have the courage to entertain.

— Emil Cioran

But, but, can we tell, *blue skies from paint*?
Not because one is necessarily all that different from the other. After all, it is not as if *blue* always existed: not that we will ever quite know if that were so because the sea seemed, showed itself as, *wine dark* to Odysseus, or if we merely hadn't yet named it *blue*.

Perhaps, the first glimpse of blue appeared when the sun burnt out Icarus' eyes; and the moment he fell into the sea, all colour changed.

Which is not to say that appearances don't matter. Far from it.
For, as Slavoj Žižek continues to ask us: « how can reality appear to itself? Because appearance means a terrible gap. Things are not directly what they are, they *appear* to themselves ... The minimum of reflexivity — appearance — is absolutely universal. For me, the lesson of quantum physics is that appearances matter — how you measure it, how things appear, determines how things are ».

So, not just *we see what we see*, in the sense that everyone — at least potentially — sees differently, but that *what is seen is precisely what we see*. Where *do you think you can tell* is not just a question of knowing, of being able to differentiate, but the very basis of knowledge itself.

Which should not surprise us.

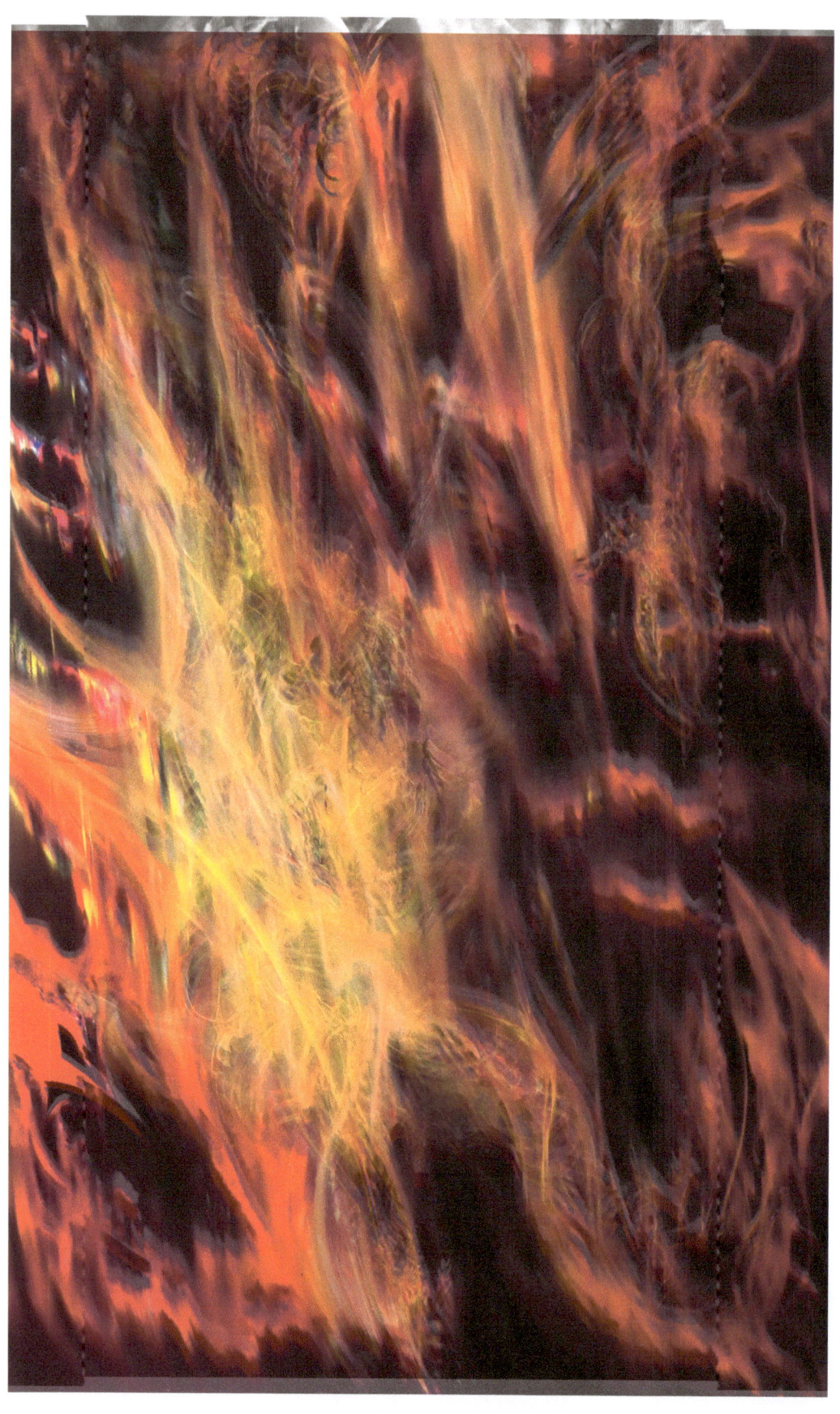

I believe in Second Chances
I believe in Second Chances

After all, *cosmetics*, the highest form of artifice, re-appearance, is of the order of the *cosmos* — has always been a question of *beauty*, of *truth*. And if art is about transformation, movement — perhaps even a shift in form of what is brought forth through *tekhnē*, by craft, into something else; brought about by the whispers of a *daemon* — it is no wonder that, returning to Slavoj once again, « art lies in the gap between the frame and the viewer ».

And, perhaps crucially, art takes place, art happens, not to the one who sees, but the one who views, who scans, who runs her eye past: where it lies — for, who ever said artifice had anything to do with truth — in its, as it is, running past.

Keeping in mind the possibility that movement can only be glimpsed at; can only be potentially seen if one is not looking too closely, too carefully. Or even, can only be seen if one is not looking — not trying to see. Not knowing what one is attempting to see.

For, if one wants to be *watching the tides flowing away*, all one can do is to be *sitting in the dock of the bay*. Nothing can, should, be said of forces, of moon cycles, of gravity — otherwise, all one will be seeing are waves. If one is attempting to attend to *tides*, particularly those that are *flowing away*, all one can do is to be *sitting* there, *wasting time*.

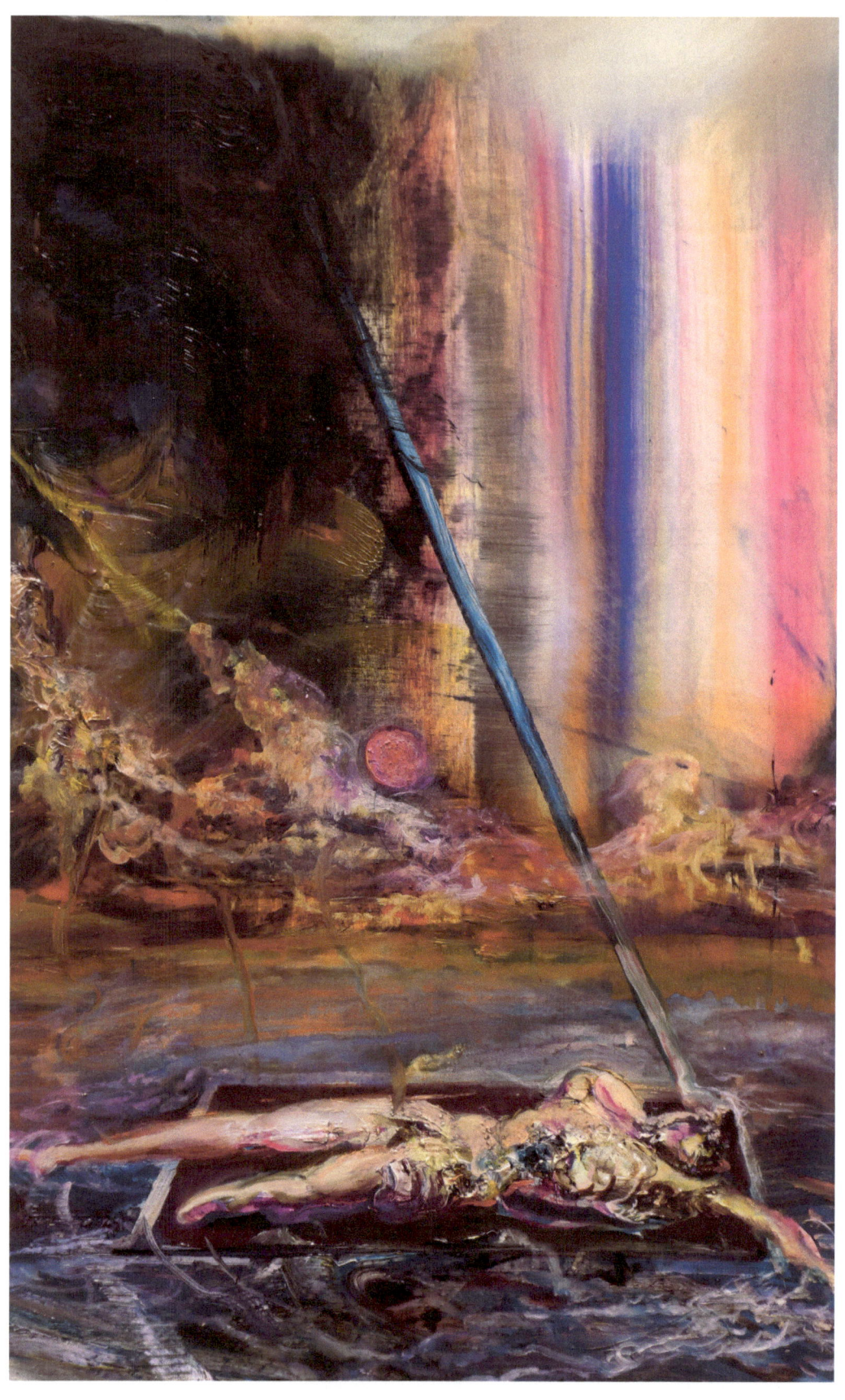

Cured and Candied

Which is not to say that art is antithetical to knowing, to knowledge, nor its antonym: but that it is a knowing that does not know, *un savoir qui ne voit pas*.

Which might well be why her owl only flies in the twilight — for, the goddess always knew that the transformation from *tekhnē* to art always happens due to the movement of the world. Not that one sees the world differently — nothing that banal — but when there is a gap between the object and what is seen. When a chair is both a chair, in all its usefulness, its purpose, but at the same time not-quite-just-a-chair; where the purposefulness of crafting this chair is somehow just *slightly beyond* its purpose: just *slightly beyond* — this gap — being nothing other than not just *un pas au-delà*, but also another name for the *chair-ness* of the chair.

> *You realize the sun doesn't go down.*
> *It's just an illusion caused by the*
> *world spinning round*
>
> — Dave Fridmann, Michael Ivins,
> Steven Drozd, & Wayne Coyne

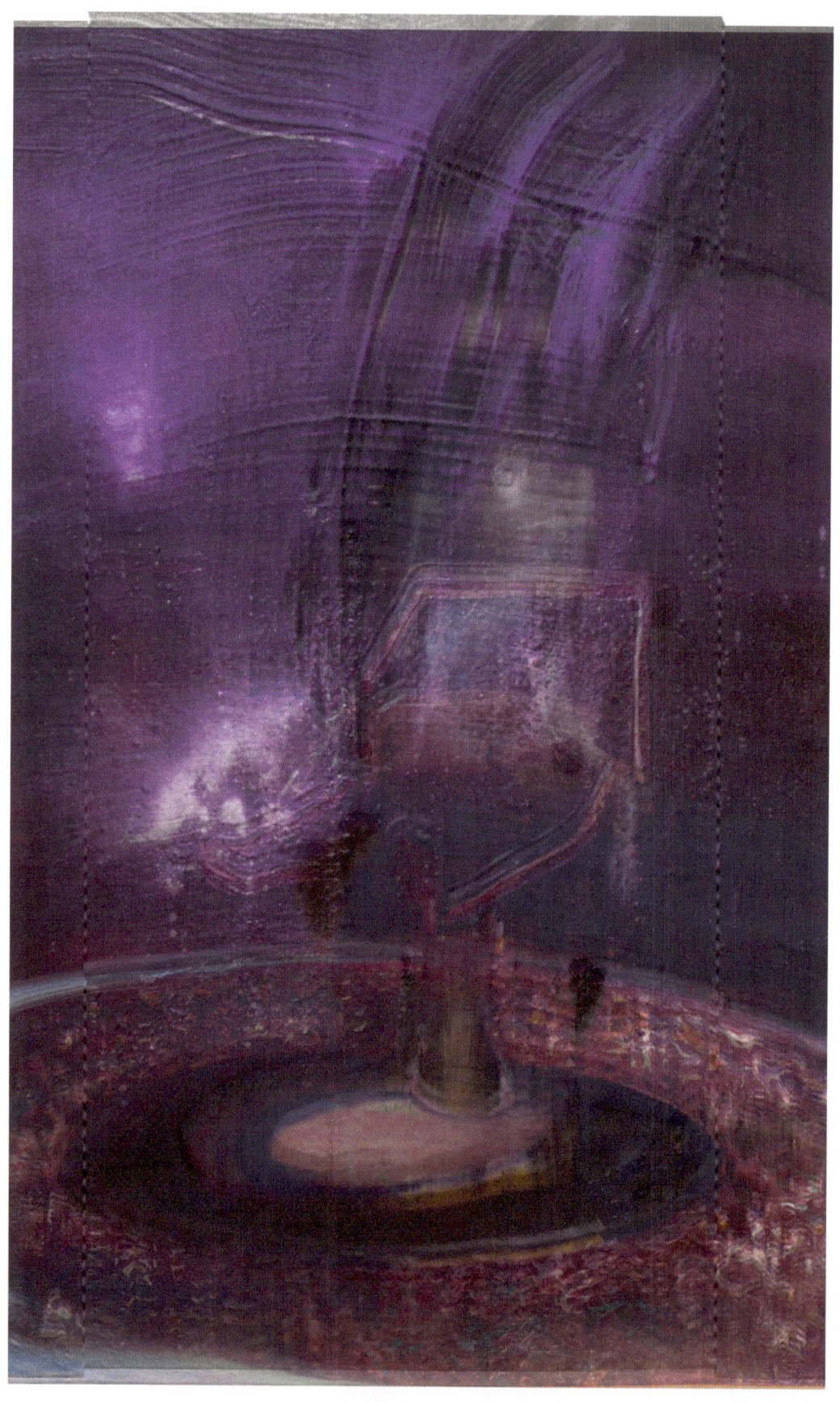

Same Time Everyday light reflection angle
Same Time Everyday light reflection angle

art: another name for a transcendence that is not transcendental, an immanent transcendence.

Which might perhaps also be why « blue skies cause us more sadness »; not because blue is any more hopeful than grey, nor due to a lack of gumption to face hope, but that what we are lacking is the courage to see that we cannot see the difference, that *we can't tell blue skies from grey.*

Yet, I do wonder what Ruben's hands see.
Perhaps nothing other than a salad for an eye

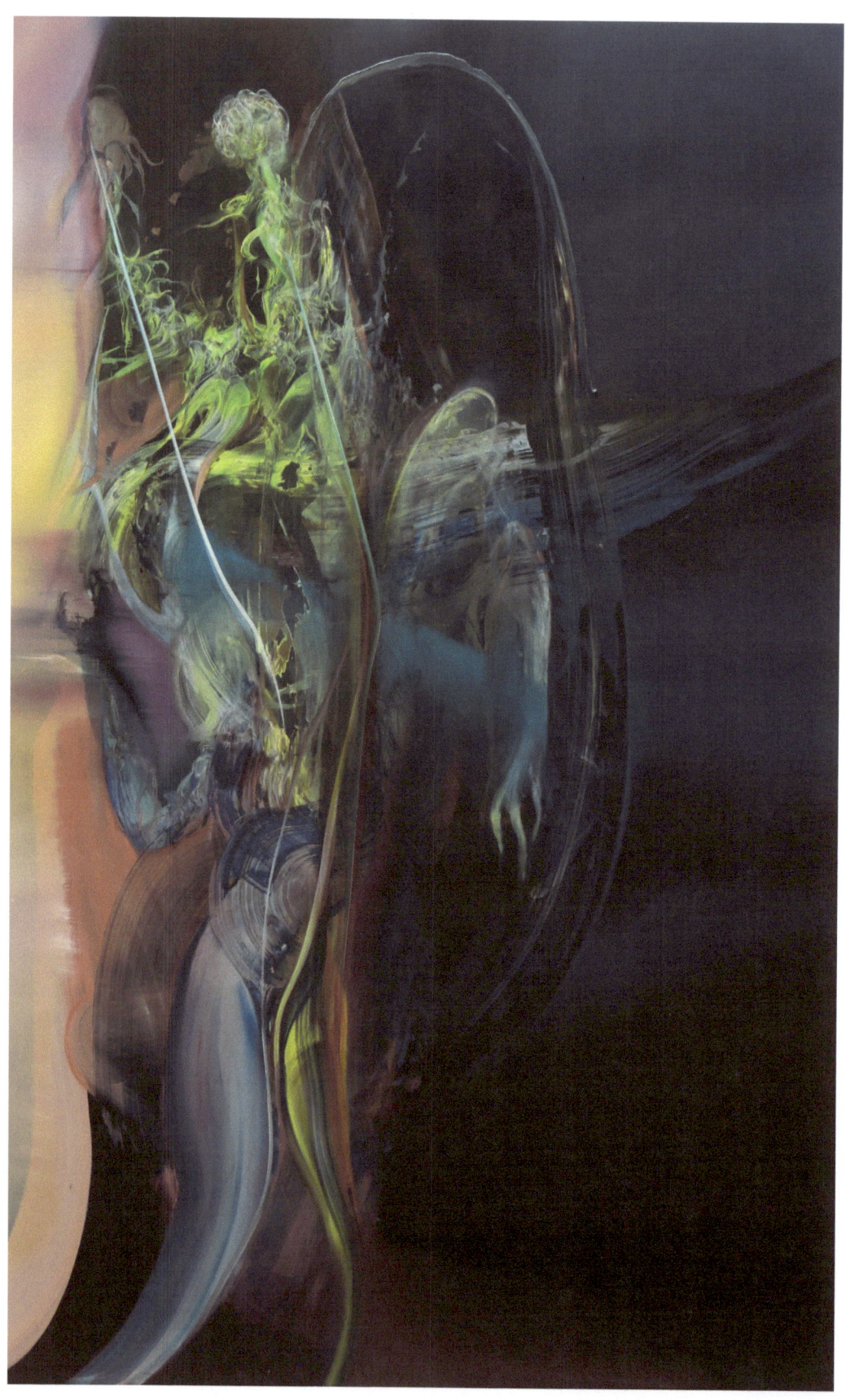

Salad for an Eye

*The Word proves
those first hearing it
as numb to understanding
as the ones who have not heard.*

— Heraclitus, Fragment 1

                                                                                               But what of images?

                    What would those « who have not heard » see?

Keeping in mind that we are being exhorted to not forget that understanding only comes to one in the second hearing — where understanding, knowing even, occurs as part of memory, happens through remembering. Where perhaps, at each second hearing, recognition comes about through realising that one has previously heard it — a realisation that *I've seen this before.*

Thus, always also bringing with it the question of a *first seeing* — of what happens in an original encounter, as it were; an *auctorial* encounter; one in which one might well be authoring the very encounter, writing that encounter itself into being. For, we should try not to forget that the very notion of *encounter* suggests — at least — the possibility of firsts, of the coming together of unknowns, of unknowability itself.

Which also means: that even as there might be, even if there is, an encounter, the two or more in that encounter might not know not just what they are encountering, but if one is even taking place.

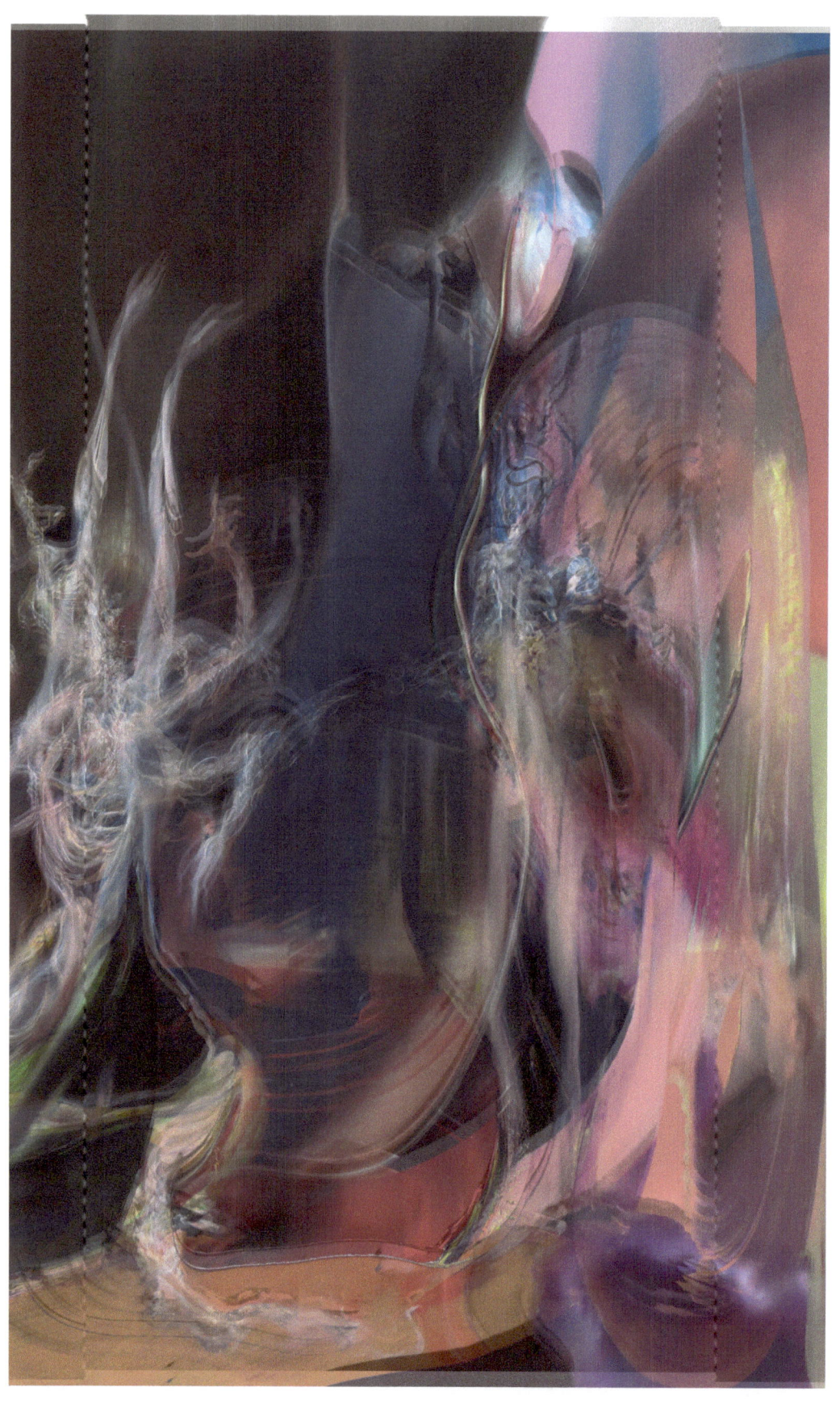

Someone Precious Rearranged
Someone Precious Rearranged

Thus, not an act.
For, that would require an *a priori* notion of the encounter in order to judge what has' to ascertain if it has, happened. But a happening: which, at best, might be known, recognised — but even this is uncertain — as it is happening.

Which also opens the possibility that *first seeings* are soundless — that they do not register aurally, if at all, with the one who catches a glimpse of them: that perhaps sound only occurs the second time, in second seeings. That sound — *insofar as sound brings with it understanding* — is

an echo.

And seeing that an echo is always already dual, a doubling of itself, sound is always already multiple.

echoes

Yet
all
things
follow
from
the
Word.

For, it is precisely only in following — not our following, but in the trailing of sound, the *second sound which follows the first* — that one can begin to catch a glimpse of the Word. And here, if one begins to doubt the possibility that an echo can bring forth something else, something new, one should try not to forget that this is precisely how Echo manages to speak with Narcissus.

Overhead the albatross hangs motionless upon the air
And deep beneath the rolling waves
in labyrinths of coral caves
The echo of a distant tide
Comes willowing across the sand
And everything is green and submarine

— Roger Waters, Richard Wright, Nick Mason, David Gilmour

However, it might not be quite so simple as listening to a sound the second time: for, one must bear in mind that repetition relies on there being a first, that the one who hears the second sound must also have heard the first. Moreover, it is only an echo — one only knows that one is hearing an echo — when one is hearing, when one thinks one has heard, both the first and second sounds.

Perhaps then, it is both that « all things follow from the Word » and, at the same time, that all knowing is in the recognition of this very *following* itself — in the « yet », as it were. And since only the one that hears — who hears both sounds — can have the possibility of recognising, of potentially knowing, this also suggests that (s)he can have no guide, no heuristic, to this recognition, to this knowing.

In this sense, (s)he is completely free in her hearing, free to hear.

That being said, one should try not to forget Jacques Derrida's reminder that « you are free, but there are rules » : in that, one is free to look, but the moment one attempts to interpret, attempts to know, one is always already bound by the laws of seeing. That one's right to look (*droit du regard*) is bound by the law (*le droit*) — confined by rules; where one's look is always also open to a right of inspection (*un droit du regard*).

One could well say the same thing of *hearing*:
that one is free to hear in any way one desires, but the moment one attempts to make anything of what one hears, one is back in the realm of the law; *un droit d'entendre*.

Keeping in mind — if we momentarily return to Echo and Narcissus — that she conveyed her thoughts to him not merely through repetition, but through omission: that each echo of his words came back to him *same same but different*; where perhaps it is not just what is echoed, but what remains silent, which brings about the possibility of their communion. Where perhaps the resistance of Echo to Hera, the resistance to power herself, is precisely through a *silent speech*.

— a secret chord —

One that might perhaps be waiting to be heard,
awaiting another hearing.

Remember everything you've seen
because everything you forget
returns to fly in the wind

— Navajo proverb

So, even when *brought before the law*, it defers judgment, turns away from being heard, utters — by not uttering — to the law, *yes, but not yet.*

For, it is sight that lets one testify, that is of the order of belief, of knowing (*savoir*) — that lets one bring before the law, that also lets one be brought before the law.

But hearing — or, more precisely, a *silent hearing* — is, quite possibly of the order of the wind, of flying (*voler*), of sails (*les voiles*), of the thief (*le voleur*).

And what drifts in the wind better than sound —
perhaps only sounds that one cannot hear. Just ask Daedalus.
Which is not to say that the sound of Icarus does not always remain with him: not in spite of, despite, the fact that he could not hear what his son was saying, uttering, screaming (*cri*) as he was falling, but precisely because it was a silent scream. And it was in, and through, the very silence that the scream writes (*écrire*) itself into him.

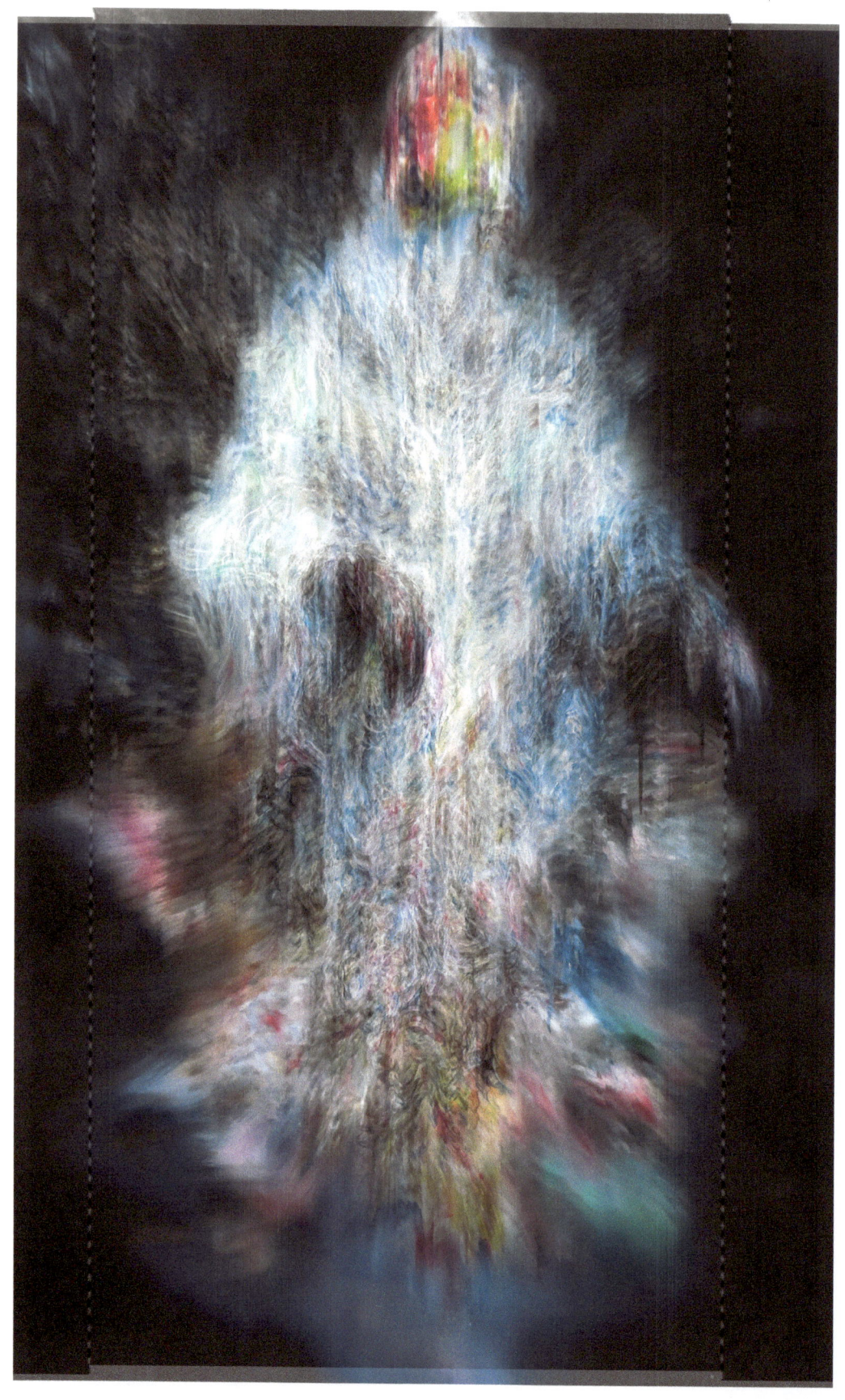

Laughter
Laughter

Writing:

or, the inscription of a silent scream. Where both the sound and the one who writes are doing nothing other than writhing in the silence of the other.

If a writer knows enough about what he is writing about, he may omit things that he knows. The dignity of movement of an iceberg is due to only one ninth of it being above water.

— Ernest Hemingway

Keeping in mind the possibility that objectivity is not antonymous to subjectivity: it is, rather, the relationship between a subject and an object, where (s)he is attempting to respond to and with an object — a relationship which tries never to forget that an object keeps its secrets; that all one can know, catch a glimpse of, is an aspect of the object ...

Or, more — perhaps only less — than that:
that all one can catch a glimpse of, is the *silence* of the object; and that *soundless sound* is precisely what one is attempting to attend to, respond with.

Writing;
or, a *name* for
an inscription of,
the attempt to inscribe,
silence.

Where what one writes, gives a name to, is a momentary
— for, once written, it is already gone —
name for silence.

*All those moments will be
lost in time, like tears in rain.
Time to die.*

— Roy Batty

Where one is doing nothing other,
one can do nothing more, than
— nor infinitely less than — to be
writing death

*Space is only noise
if you can see*

— Nicolas Jaar

I feel like I'm painting blind as I tread between the deliberate and the spontaneous. Much of the marks are made with my fingertips; shaped with solvent, through erasure; with dust flicked away from the surface, sanded away, letting them take flight. After which, I put glazes — veils — over these open wounds to settle them into the surface once more.

— Ruben Pang

I would like to begin right away by excusing myself — for, I know very little of what I am about to attempt to write on, very little of what I write:

Even as this might be an excuse that perhaps comes too late: for, even as I am making it, it is already made, can only be made, in writing. Which is not to say that I am attempting to disavow what I have written, what I will write, but that perhaps all writing lies in excusing — in requesting a pardon, in asking for forgiveness.

Bearing in mind — for, this should always be a burden — that one can only confess to one, to another, who already knows. For, confession is not a matter of knowledge: one confesses as if the other already knows of the transgression. Whether this is true — both the confession and the transgression — is beside the point: otherwise, it is only a matter of revealing, of telling. Confession lies in asking: regardless of whether the other knows if (s)he has been wronged — quite possibly even if either the request, or the matter of being wronged, is a lie.

And this is why confessions can only be a ritual, take place through rites: for, it is not so much a matter of what is being confessed, but the fact that a confession takes place, that one has confessed. Thus, confessions are strictly speaking meaningless: it is not their signification that matters, but the significance of their occurance.

Especially if one is attempting to write as a response to: for, as even as I attempt to respond to Ruben's paintings in all of their possibilities, one can — I can — never be certain if I am writing on, writing about, or writing over, his works. Even worse: all of my words are, my writing is, haunted by the possibility that all I am doing is making Ruben's works say what I want them to say; bringing them forth in order that they, conjuring them such that they, speak for me;

prosopopoeia

So perhaps:
not just that each writing (*écriture*) is writhing in the possibility that it is saying something other than it should, is struggling with the fact that it is speaking over, silencing, what it is attempting to speak for, but that in order for writing to maintain a certain responsibility, to maintain the possibility that it is responding, it would have to always also be erasing what it writes.

>Where each scribble, *scribere*, not only scratches into, stains — paints — the surface on which it is writing, but also scratches out, tears, opens, runs the possibility of wounding, even as it is tearing, crying out (*cri*).

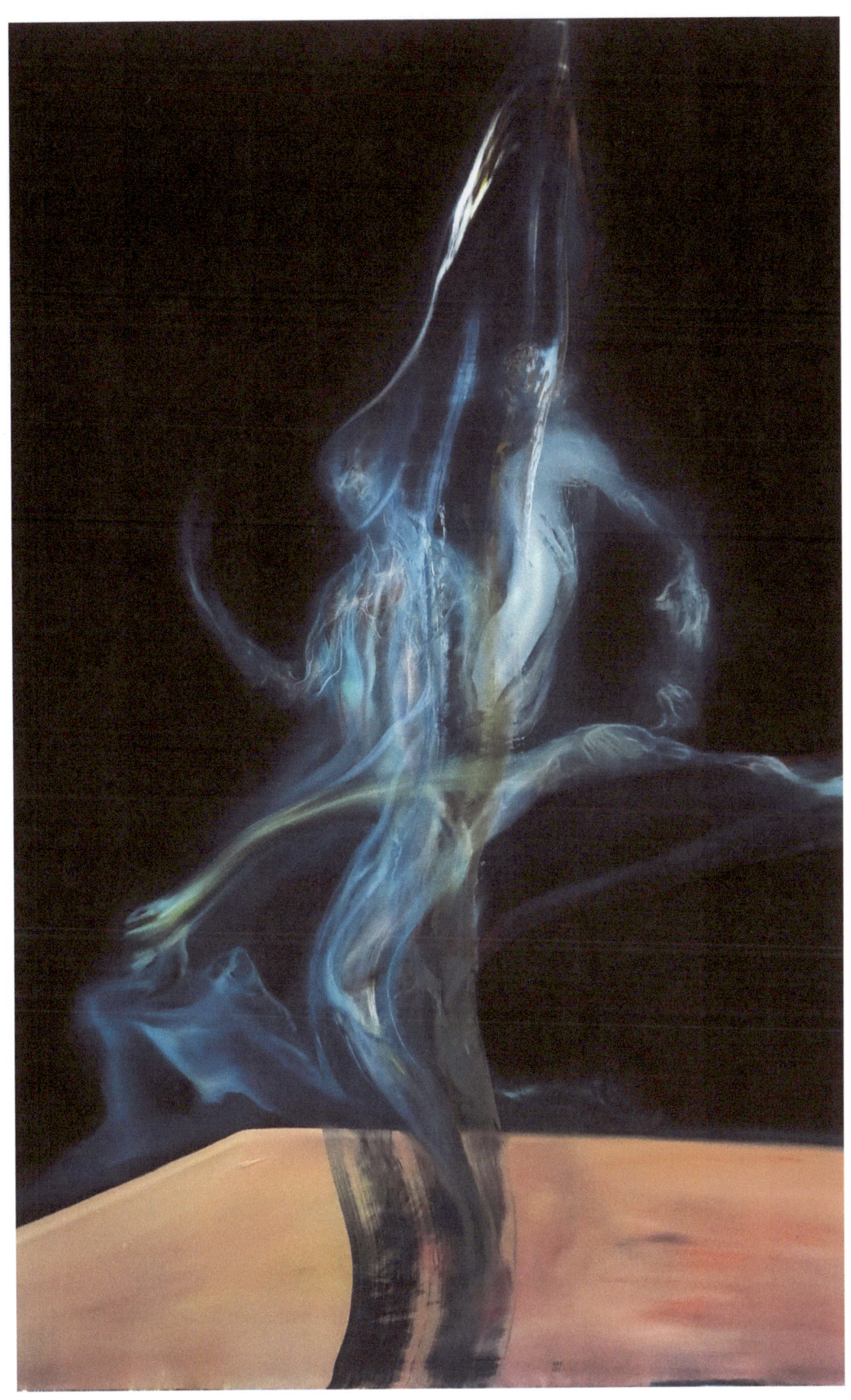

Fear so long what passes quickly

A re-quest: a doubled quest.
Where doubling over not only repeats, goes back over, but is always also haunted by the first quest, the initial question. Not just what is said, nor if what is being said has any veracity, but a more primordial question — *qui parle*. Where perhaps, every moment of trying to capture = to know, to grasp, to comprehend, to take into one's hand, *prendre* = is to always already render it dead. But where perhaps, it is love, *philia*, in its unknowability — in its refusal to claim the other for itself = which maintains the space for life. Where all the one who loves might be able to say is *qui parle* — but, without ever needing to know who the who of the speech is:

Where perhaps, all that the one who writes can say is — without knowing either what (s)he says, nor even who the I who writes is =

I love you: I work at understanding you to the point of not understanding you, and there, standing in a wind, I don't understand you. Not understanding in a way of holding myself in front and of letting come. Transverbal, transintellectual relationship, this loving the other in submission to the mystery. (It's accepting, not knowing, forefeeling, feeling with the heart.) I'm speaking in favour of non-recognition, not of mistaken cognition. I'm speaking of closeness, without any familiarity.

— Hélène Cixous

always already = and perhaps only possible = in the words of another, the other.

::: whereas a painter: perhaps all (s)he is — are her hands. all (s)he has = perhaps all (s)he is — are her hands.

For, (s)he is always blind: either to her object, or to her canvas. And all that she paints is made in blindness. Or perhaps: where it is only her hands that see, that can see, which see for her.

But what exactly they see, might remain veiled from her: perhaps even from us — even though we, even as we, see what has been painted. Where perhaps, it is only the painting that bears witness to the painting which has happened. Whether it sees what her hands see, have seen, remains though quite possibly to be seen.

I throw pure pigments onto the wet surface towards the end of the painting ::: I think of it as leaving some parts of the composition to chance, and I fantasize myself as a shaman blessing the work …

= Ruben Pang

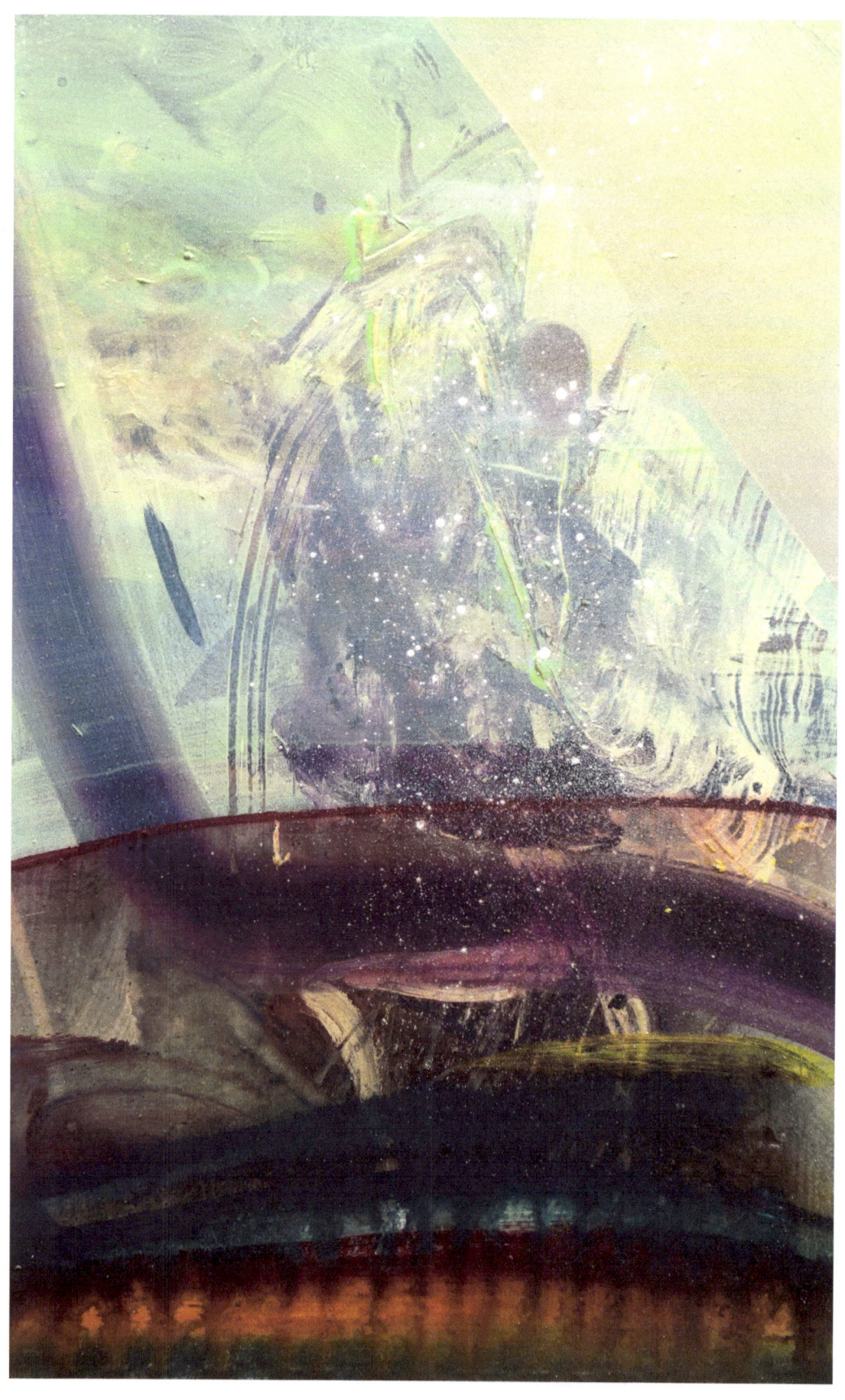

Hypnagogic Visions

to touch — to see

Trying never to forget Jean-Luc Nancy's reminder that « it is space that is first needed to touch » : which opens the possibility that there is a gap between seeing and touching. Where what is seen-touched, touched-seen, is quite possibly nothing other than space itself. Where perhaps, the moment touching takes place, nothing can be seen: where touch happens in the *not-seen*, cannot be seen.

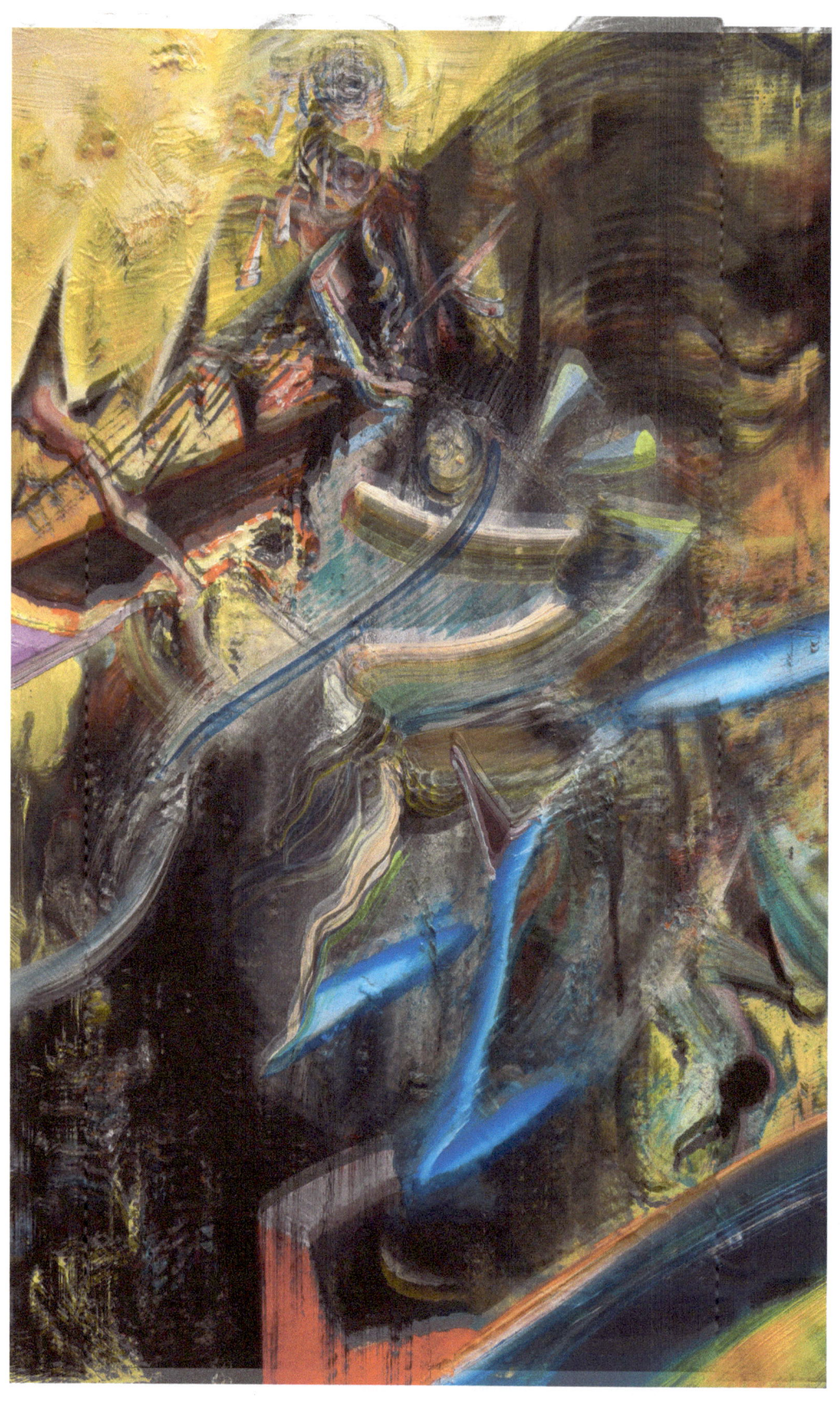

The Pneumatic Body
The Pneumatic Body

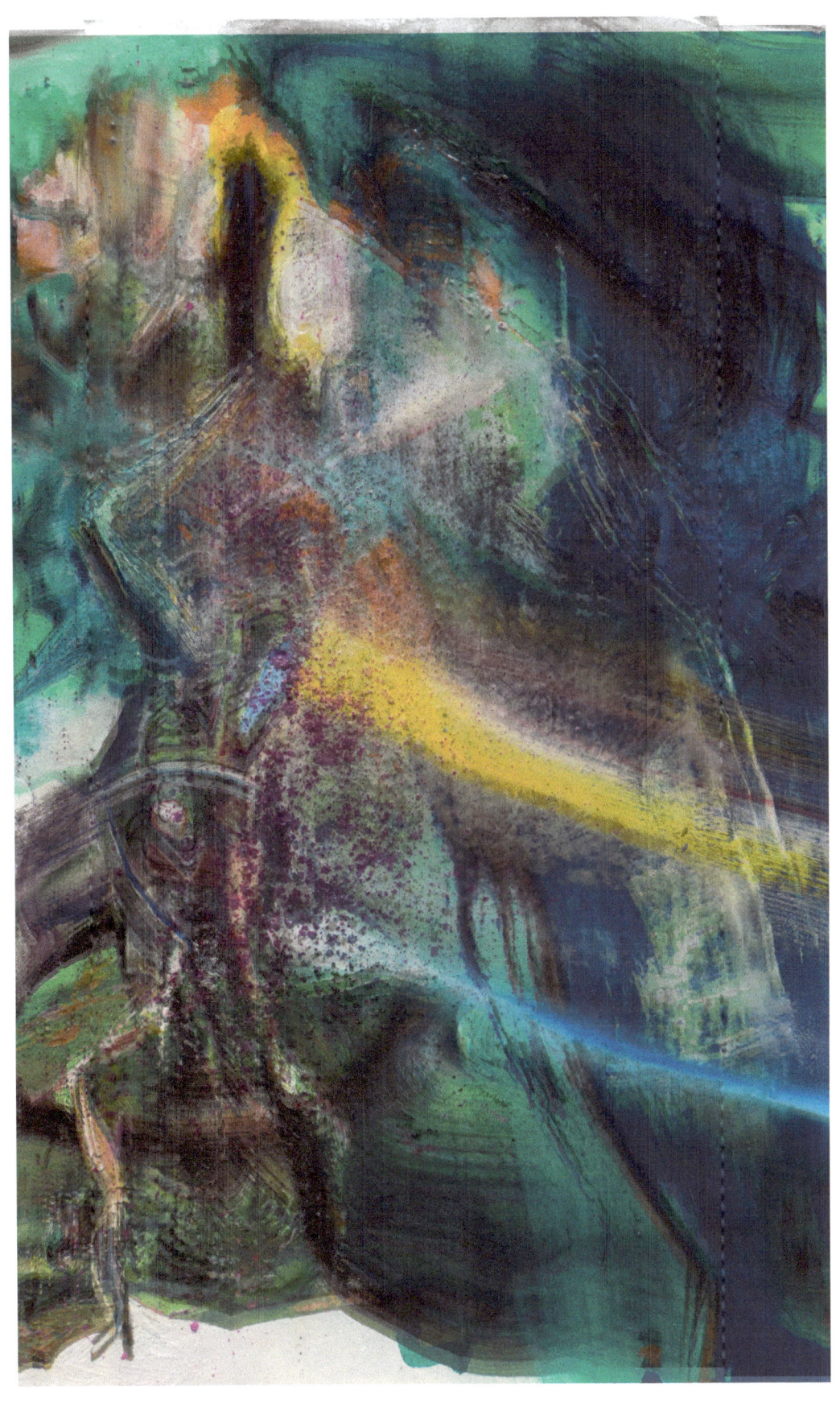

As I Drown, The Water Laughs
As I Drown, The Water Laughs

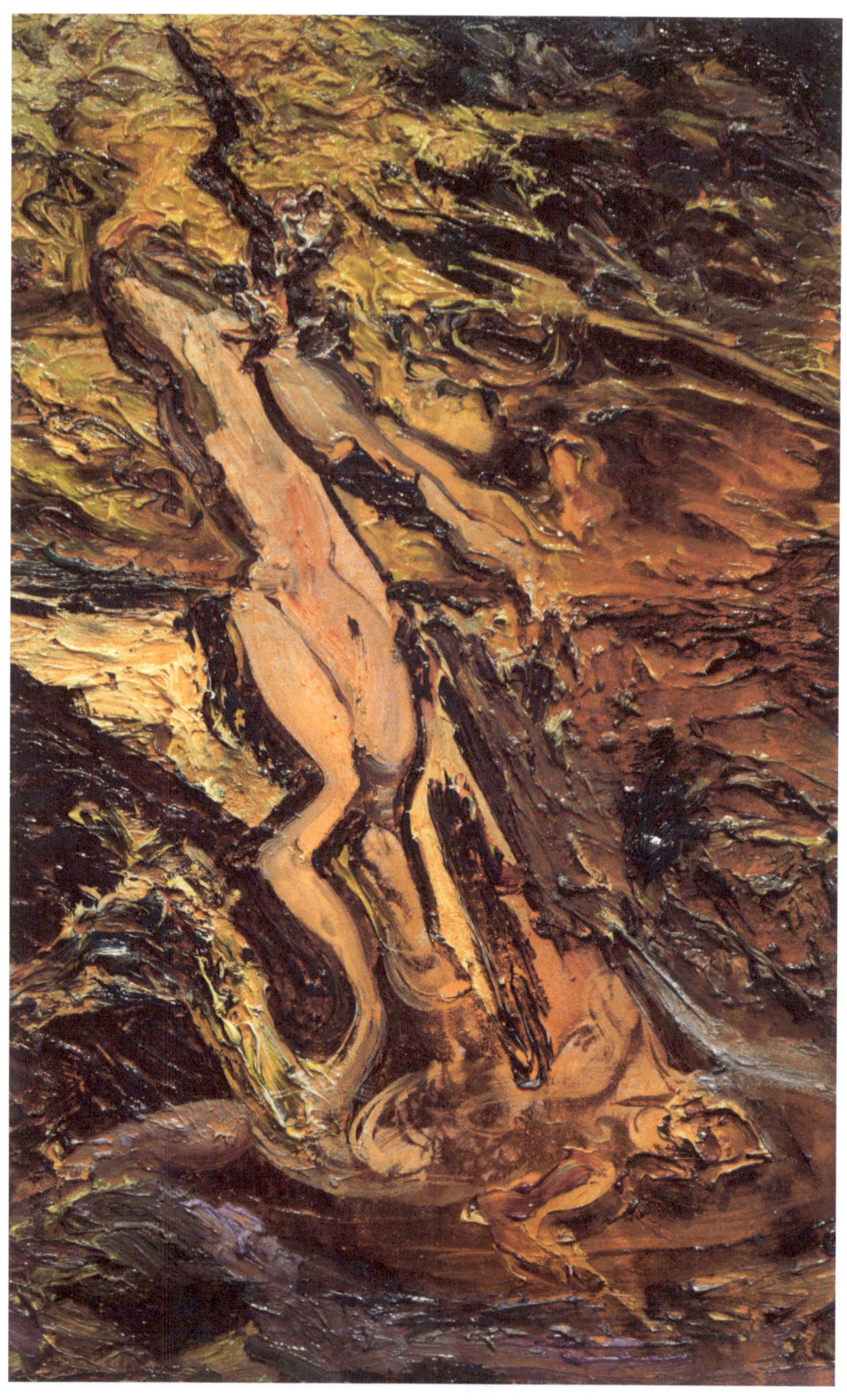

From My Milk White Veins

— a secret touch
quite possibly, a sacred touch —

Where skin is nothing other than the site of the *blind touch*:

Thus, *touching*, insofar as anything can be known (*savoir*) of it, is always already in the *to-come*, in the possibility of touching — the scene of the touch always already remaining behind a veil (*un voile*): And which quite possibly takes flight, flies away (*s'envole*) — on a sail (*une voile*), floating away into the wind — the moment one attempts to touch it:

Where all that can be known of it, is that it (*ça*) has happened: a knowing by way of an acknowledgement (*une connaissance*); of which sight has long already left the building — at best, perhaps a seeing that is to-come, a *to-see*, where perhaps all that might have happened is that *it sees* (*ça voit*).

And where perhaps what is seen only lies in the moment just before the touch: in between the *about to touch* and *touched* … in the gerund, as it were.

Where, all attempts to steal (*voler*) it only leaves us with its shroud:

Which might perhaps be a lesson of the allegory of the cave: that, it is not so much that we should be looking out of the cave — for, staring at the sun only leads to more blindness, to complete blindness even — but that one should make better shadows. Which might well be why Socrates or Plato — the two quite possibly remaining indistinguishable, shadows of each other — were suspicious of artists, of art itself: for, what else is artifice but the making of beautiful shadows:

Part of the secret is gentleness ::: with fingers you caress the skins of the painting

— Ruben Pang

*My dad always said to me: leave some dirt. My mentor Nicola Samori and I have a motto: **dirty but warm**. I always wanted to paint the way Jimmy Page plays the guitar: slightly sloppy, as if the strings oxidized from its own tears as the guitar laughed, screamed, and cried.*

— Ruben Pang

Well it goes like this: the fourth, the fifth
The minor fall, the major lift

— Leonard Cohen

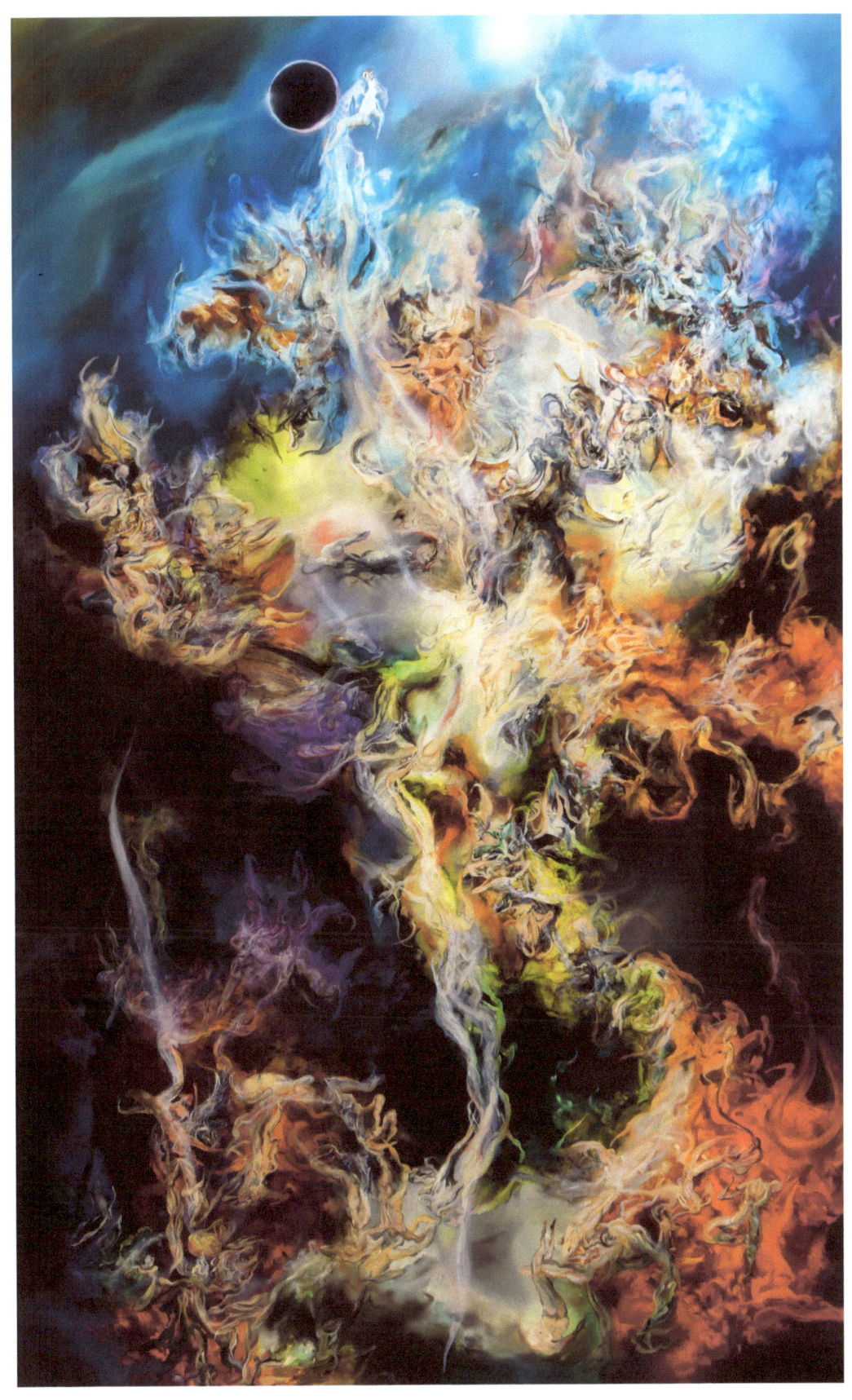

In the Shadows of the Flies We've Become

In the shadows of the flies we've become,'
she seemed to whisper to me, I hope at me, hopefully only to me; even as this will ensure not only that I am the only one who might be hearing this, but that I will never be able to say if it were ever said, let alone if she said it, if I ever heard it, or if I have only been hearing myself hear it.

For, one should try not to forget that to begin to attend to something, one must also cease one's attention from everything else: that one must attempt to tune oneself to that which one believes one is listening to — that one believes is calling one to listen to it — whilst ignoring, turning away from, detuning oneself from, all else.

Or, as Werner Hamacher might say, *listening entails ceasing to hear*.

Which means that to attend to, in attempting to attend to, each painting, each piece, I have to listen to one — enact a *caesura* — whilst ceasing to hear any of the others, to cease hearing painting itself, to withdraw from perhaps even attempting to tune in to Ruben himself.

But even as one has to listen to the call of the painting — to tune one self to the call, to recognise that there is a calling that is taking place — it is not as if one can ever quite be sure if one is listening to a call or if there is a call only because one is hearing it as such. Thus, even as *hearing* ceases, listening is quite possibly haunted by hearing, by the whispers of hearing, by the spectres of *here* in hearing: in that only in the space, place, that one has heard, that one thinks that one hears, is there this moment that *one calls* listening.

Where listening is not just a cutting off, a cut in hearing, but that the naming of it as listening is the very enactment of this cut — where the cut itself lies precisely in the moment that the very thing that one is attempting to attend to catches one's attention: a moment — a *now*, if you prefer — that is always already future-anterior; once recognised, once listened to, always already in memory, but always also in the *to-come*, as a potential, in awaiting.

Where perhaps, it is the gap between — even if this space only exists within the very *ceasing* — that one is attempting to tune oneself to. Which also means that there is no object — in the precise sense of *no thing* — to which the attunement is occuring: thus, not an act, but quite possibly only an attempt.

An attempt in attending:
en attendant.

Where one cannot say anything with respect to what or who one is awaiting — only that one is waiting.

And where, what is named — what we *call* whatever it is we think we might have been awaiting — is nothing other than a name for waiting itself:

Godot

the paintings of Ruben Pang.

the painter whom we call Ruben Pang.

same same but different.

Where the difference lies in nothing other than what is *same same*. Which opens the possibility that difference, that differences, can lie beyond our cognition; be outside of, remain exterior to, our knowledge; that what we know is bound by our phenomenological finitude. That, as Socrates, or Plato — the two remaining not just entangled but in a dance of sameness and difference, sameness in their difference; perhaps indifferent to their sameness — has taught us: to truly know we have to be inspired; struck from elsewhere. But since the divine is always already *un pas au-delà* — both beyond one, outside of one; and, at the same time, potentially within one, from one — there is no way of knowing if one is inspired or not, if one is hearing the whispers of the *daemon* or merely *voices* in one's head.

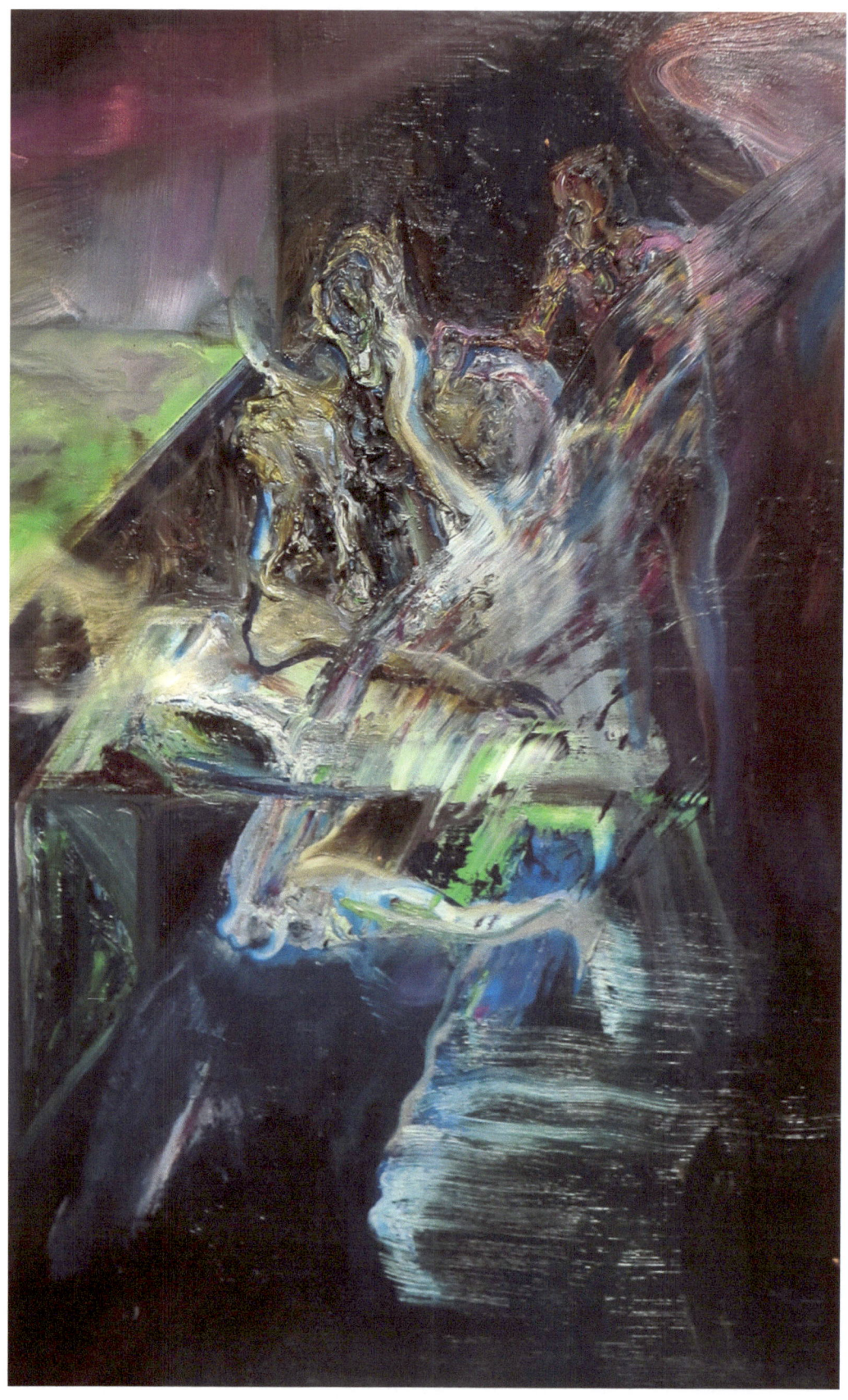

Pastoral Care

And whenever we hear the phrase, one should also try not to forget that *same* appears twice: as a pair, in tandem, as a duo. And here, one might perhaps consider the possibility that the duality, the doubling of the *same*, draws attention to the fact that something can only be different when there is another, something else, to be different from. Which is not to say that difference itself, difference only, relies on another; however, without an other — even if this other is itself at another moment, situation, context — there cannot be any difference. Thus, *same* is like *same* but is not necessarily the *same*; a duality that continues dueling whilst never ceasing to be — cutting — enacting a *caesura* on being, a duo.

Which suggests that any statement that is made on an object — even if one is attending to it, attempting to respond to it — is not only fraught with a potential error of interpretation, it runs the risk of not only bearing little or no likeness to what it attempts to speak on, write on, comment on, but might well always already be different to itself, indifferent to what it is attempting to say.

Much like reading, which is — as we read from Italo Calvino — a « going toward something that is about to be, and no one yet knows what it will be ».

	of pieces
Much like titles	of paintings
	of people

frames:
which not only enframe, but quite possibly always also frame, accuse one of what one has not necessarily done.

So, even as one might say — perhaps she might say —
there are no misunderstandings in nature ...

... this might quite possibly be due to the possibility that there are always also no understandings.

... to listen, to really listen, is a promise to not forget that which cannot remain ...

— James Batcho

For, forgetting has no object.

Thus, not only can one not know if forgetting is in every moment of remembering, in memory, knowing — in knowledge itself — but that one can never detect its presence, ever even know if it is there. Which is precisely why it *cannot remain* — for, there is no thing to leave behind. Even if it were there, were always already there.

Where all one can listen to — listen out for — is a promise: to do nothing other than to listen.

Painting leads to thought and then leaves it behind. The space of painting is a passageway. By trusting the painting as true you become a witness to events that you didn't experience directly ...

— Bracha L. Ettinger

She sounded like an angel when she cried

— CocoRosie

For Jesus himself testified, that a prophet hath no honour in his own country.

— John 4:44

Give me the first number that comes to mind, into your mind, my friend ...

— Jeremy Fernando

Four point four four

— Ruben Pang

Voir, c'est croire ;
mais sentir, c'est être sûr

— Le Marquis de Sade

Yes, but being sure of nothing
other than of feeling itself, that
one may have felt.

Passacaglia 2 — Pitch

The grains set alight previously unwatched
Waves of startling pursuits and convictions
Persuasion may take more painless expectation
Than first cast out to set the tone

A night seeing nothing but shelled voices
Echoing across widened floors
Catching sight of the dews of completion
Bridles and dovetails make right

This stretched surface that will hold
Retained fevered mists of breathy triumphs
Like a neighing in the palace of reason
Eating the glass he called silence[2]

The path of refusal doubles as the scraped
Boot yard of the still to be unearthed
Appetite for beauty devouring
The clarion calls of unreason

Lim Lee Ching

[2] cf: Tomas Tranströmer

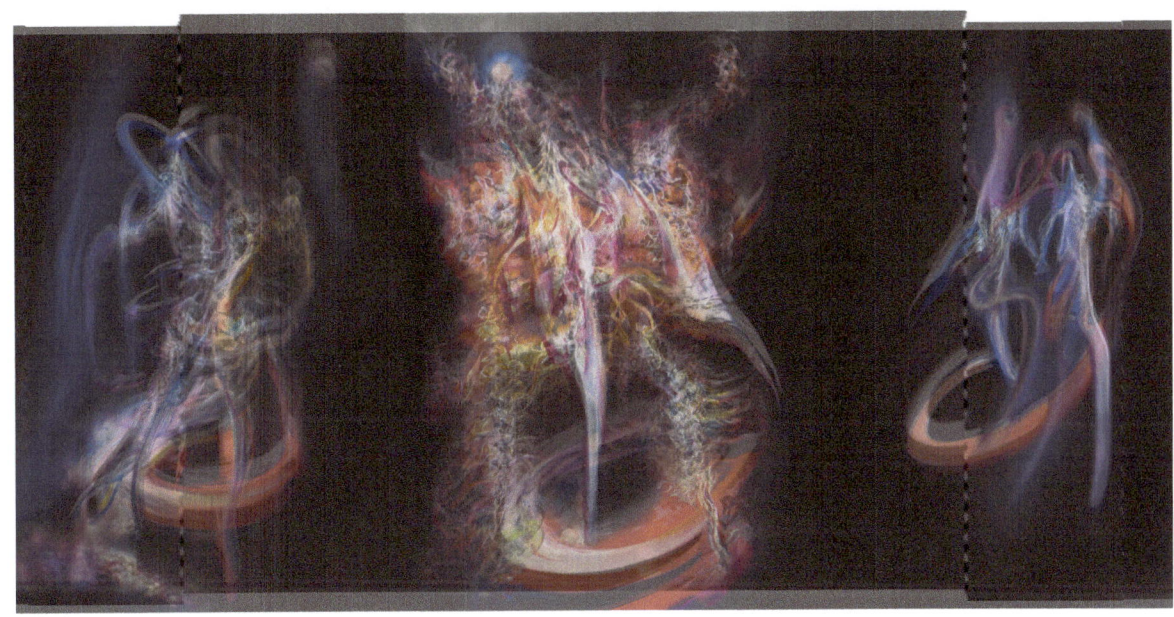

The Totalitarian Sun
The Totalitarian Sun

l'insurrection du sable

Sand.
He sands. One might even say that without the sand, without sanding, there is nothing he can say. *C'est-à-dire, sans le sable, il n'y a pas de peintre qui s'appelle Ruben Pang.* Where, all that he paints, all that he says, all that he says through his painting, could be said to be sandy; not just — because it is — coated with sand, but that it is standing on sand.

On foundations   that shift
                             that slide
                             that move

Or, more than that: without sand, not only is there no painter whom we can call, who we can name, Ruben Pang, there is no painting itself. Not in general — that would be silly — but no painting of the one, from the one, that we anoint Ruben Pang, no painting that we can invoke as a painting of Ruben Pang.

Where perhaps, what is Rubenesque about Ruben Pang might be nothing other than sand itself.

And here, we should try not to forget that foundation is precisely what allows us to apply cosmetics — which is to say, it is what we build not just our camouflage upon, but always also our *cosmos*; that is to say, *beauty itself*.

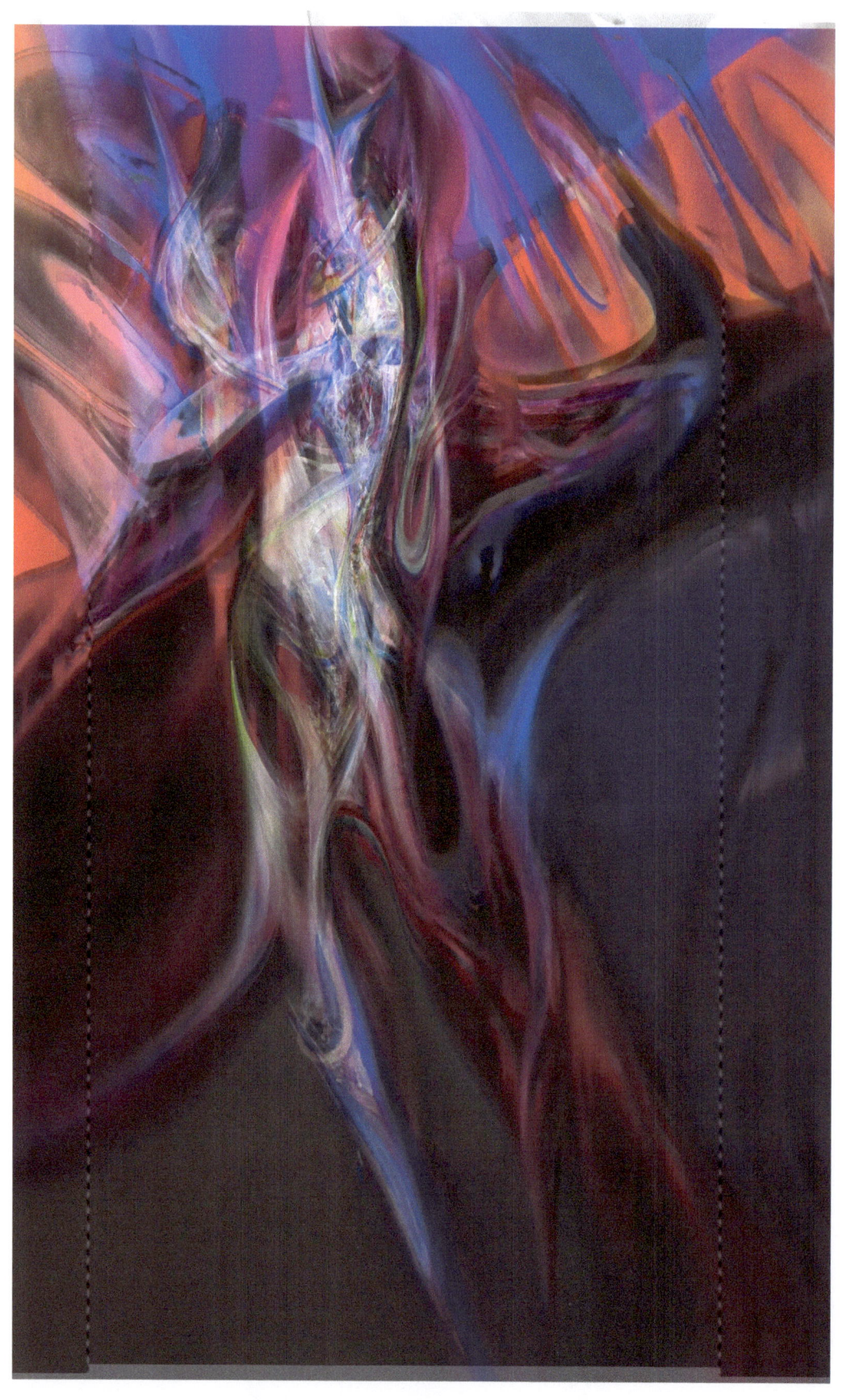

Pink Eye Athletics
Pink Eye Athletics

And what else is beauty than the whole, the round: where what gives the starkness of Ruben's paintings, what gives the painting's — what gives his — severity its roundedness, is what rises from the alkyd, what resurrects from the touch between the alkyd and aluminium, perhaps even the canvas, whilst mingling in the oil and varnish.

Bearing in mind that to touch requires two; even if one touches oneself (*je me touche*), even if it is between one and one's self, between *I* and *me*.

Thus, always a space between; whilst trying never to forget that space — for, it is precisely what lies between the things one can see. And thus, one quite possibly cannot speak of it, if one can even posit it as *it*.

And even if one takes a position on space, attempts to respond to it, space itself might well be telling — be showing us — lies; might well be made in a Hollywood basement.

And it's so hard to talk about paintings, because to be honest, there is very little to talk about. I think it would be adding unnecessarily into something ... I'd risk stating the obvious ... I personally refrain from trying to translate it into words ...

— Ruben Pang

And, where perhaps attempting to speak about spaces is always already a speaking into a space, into space itself: a launching of sound into a nothing — an in-between things, so even if not a thing onto itself, always already *with* things — which echoes, scatters, spreads. Where all one can do is attempt to tune oneself, adjust one's receptors, to traces of this invisible speech.

Which is not to say that nothing is left behind: for, sound can draw itself, can make a note (*une remarque*) for us, leave a mark to be seen, quite possibly for one to bear witness to;

       particularly in sand.

And, to speak of sand is to speak of dust; but not just what is dusted off, removed — for, the moment it moves, it always also brings with it the possibility of settling; and even as it moves, it might well be about to settle, where each movement is potentially the one just before it settles. Like cinders; remainders of a flame; reminders that something was once alight, that there once was light.

Thus, it is also to speak of what cannot be spoken of.

Of what is — at least potentially is — not there.

Or, at best, it is an attempt to speak of a trace; to speak of seeing what either cannot be seen, or is seen only because it lets itself be glimpsed. In either case, it might be impossible to know if what is seen precedes the seeing, awaiting the possibility of being seen — keeping in mind that potentiality always also brings with it the *impotentiality of the potentiality-not-to-be* — or if it only appears at the moment of being seen, after the fact of the seeing, as it were.

Where perhaps what is left, what remains — the shadows left by one's hands (*les mains*), that are quite possibly also on one's hands — is the dust of the painting, the painting that is dust.

For, to sand, sand down,
is both to take away and attempt to affix — to allow to fix itself, even as it is always also prefixed by the possibility of detachment. Not just a removal, but a falling over by itself.

Thus, always also a question of what returns,
comes back at us, rises, surges (*insurgere*);
even as one is attempting to sweep one's   hands
    paintbrush
    sandpaper

Not that one would be able to differentiate,
at least with any certitude, exactly what is being
swept aside, at any given moment.

For, we should try never to forget Hélène Cixous' reminder that the sweeper, « *le balayeur passe le balai entre le vivant et le mourant. La vie essuie la mort, le balai longe le bord de la fin, en flairant le ras du sol, il est maigre et raide, c'est tout ce qui reste d'un flexible massif de genêt* ».

Keeping in mind that both *living* and *dying* are not phases; for, even as *life* and *death* are terms, might be nouns, they are names for the unknown, the unknowable; names naming nothing except the fact that they are naming. So, even as we might be attempting to fill it with meaning, with signification, perhaps though a little force-feeding — for, *gorging is never gentle* — it remains ahead of us, or perhaps behind us, like a shadow; never quite within our grasp, prehension, certainly comprehension, always perhaps leaving us in, mayhaps even filling us with, apprehension.

Which might well be why it holds our attention.

Which might well be why Ruben Pang's paintings call out to us, grab us, call us to attention.

For, as Martin Heidegger never lets us forget, *anxiety* is the very condition of thought, of thinking, itself.

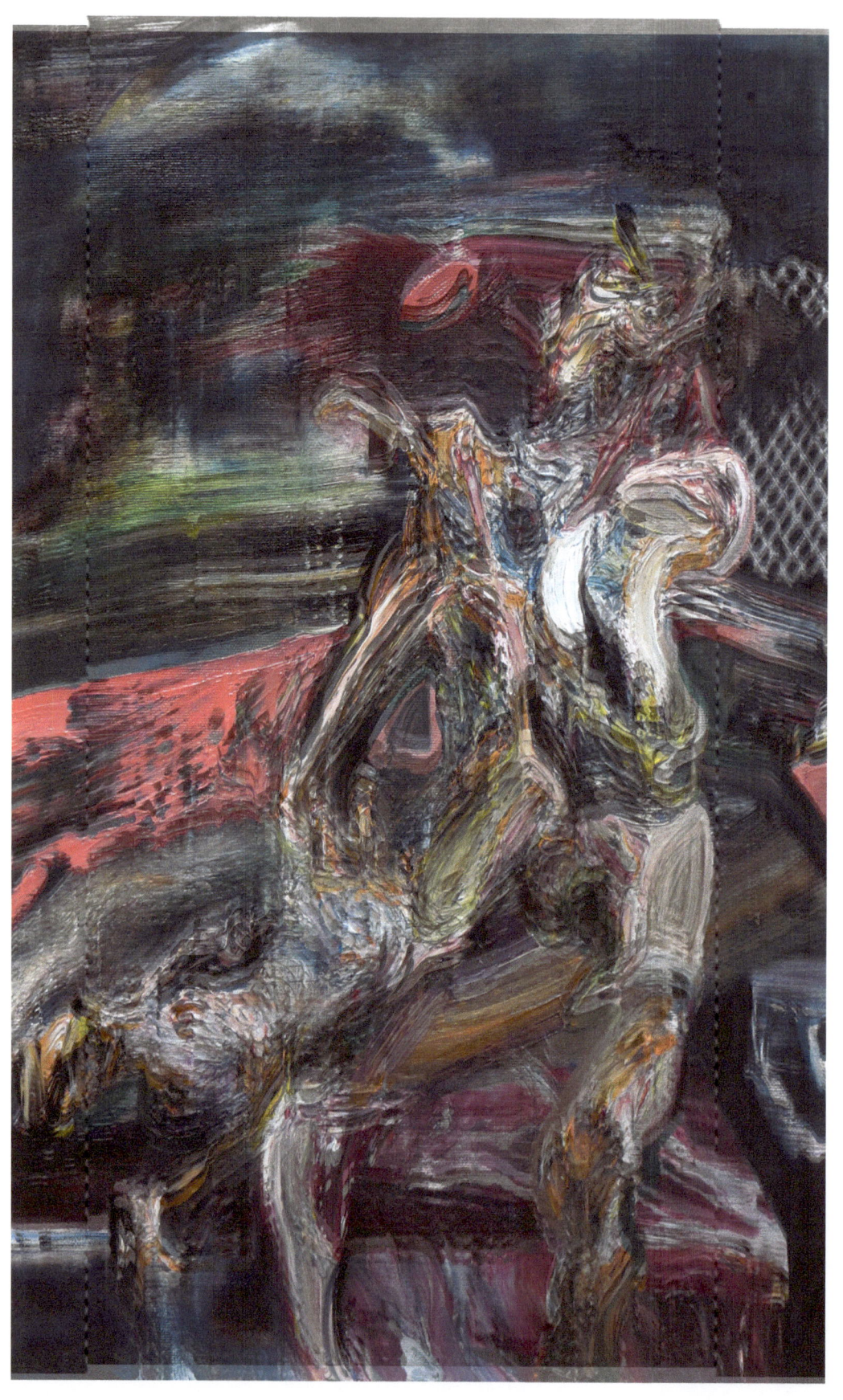

Gorging will never be gentle
Gorging will never be gentle

Which is not to say that everything is swept away: for, even as it may be, might well become, dust in the wind, we should attempt to hold on to the reminder, the hopeful promise, that my dear friend Adel Abdessemed posits when he says, « *les balayeuses sont les derniers peintres du monde* ».

Painters that paint at the very moment that they *sniff the ground*; in the instant they *pass their brooms between living and dying*, where life wipes death, sweeps along the edge of the end.

Where in looking, attempting to look, in my attempt to attend to Ruben Pang, one has the feeling that he is *cradling me bravely*; for, he knows all too well the lesson that Jean-Luc Nancy leaves us with; that « language is radically improper when faced with painting ... Painting doesn't speak. There's a silence where painting's concerned, an *absolute muteness* ».

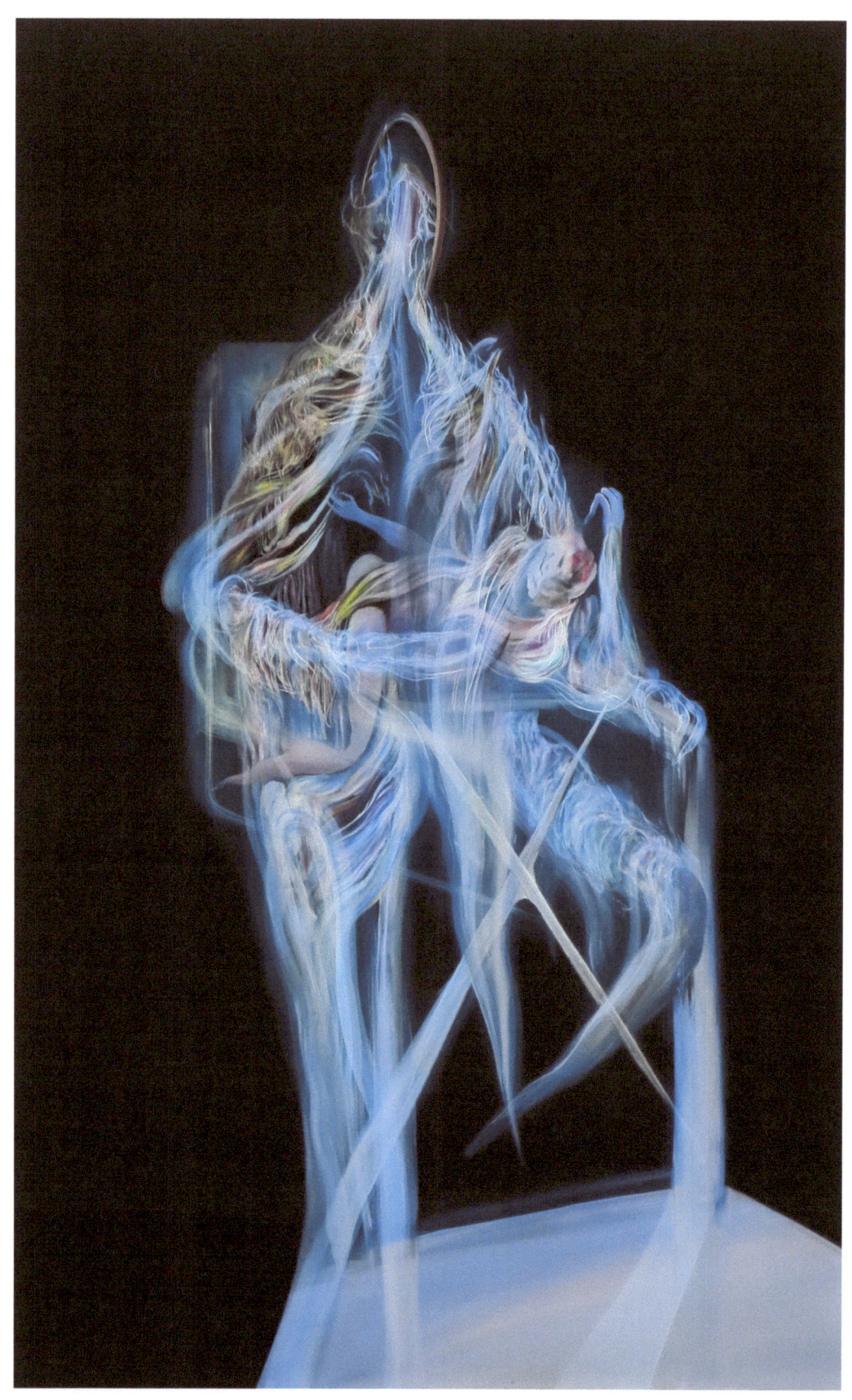

Cradle Me Bravely

And where all one might be doing — where what I might be doing; might have no choice but to do — is to be speaking over the painting as one is attempting to let it speak: in a *role reversal*, as it were. But where — if one is attempting to maintain a space for the painting to speak — what is speaking is not a sound, but a sound that doesn't speak; a silence of *absolute muteness*.

And where perhaps all that can be heard
— where all one can attempt to attend to, tune in to —

is the sweeping of   the broom
                                      the brush
                                      the reed

The sounds of what perhaps touches — even makes — the painting; of which the painting is what, all that, remains. Where all that is heard is the sound of the absent, perhaps even *the sound of absence* itself.

And here, one should try to bear in mind that even if one is — I am — running the risk of speaking for the painting, am risking the possibility of ruining the painting whilst attempting to respond to it, the very attempt at responding is an opening of the possibility of a relationship with it. And each time one opens oneself to the potentialities of a relation, of a response, of responding, one is also opening oneself to the possibilities — and all the dangers — of being touched by *eros*.

Where one might end up being *tied to a kitchen chair, in a broken throne whilst (s)he cuts your hair* …

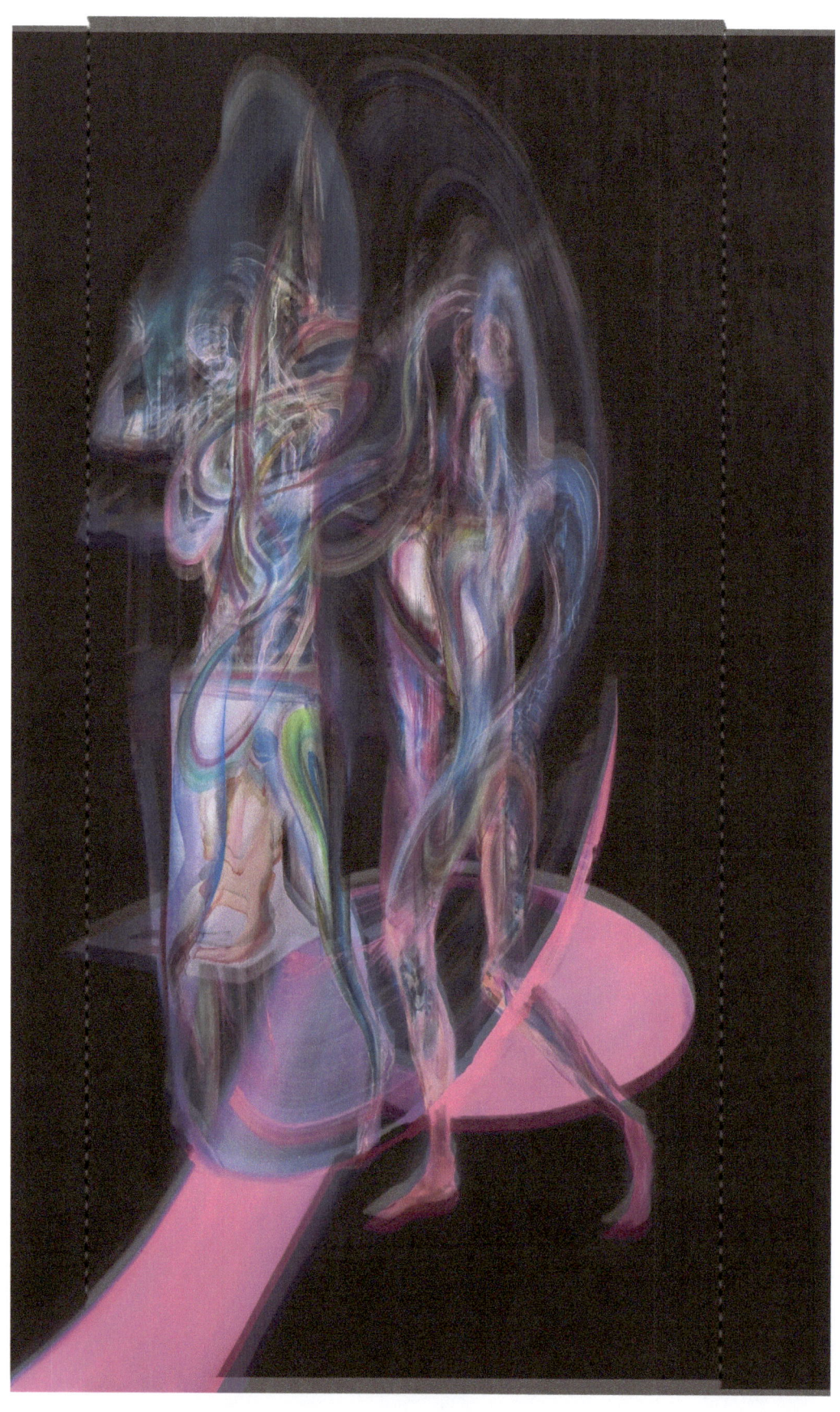

Eromenos — Role Reversal

But, at the same time, it is perhaps only in this manner — by opening oneself to the whispers of something beyond — that one might catch a glimpse of a speech that might be speaking

— in the voice of the painting —

certainly not that of Ruben Pang:
for, even as it might have been his hands that were,
his touch that is, involved in the painting,
in painting the paintings, he is silent.

And where, as Yves Klein might say,
the painting is only the witness who saw what happened.

Which is not to say that Ruben Pang has naught to do with this, any of this, perhaps even all of this.

Far from it:

For, even if one posits that the painting might not have anything to do with the one who paints, it is still the hands of Ruben Pang who make the mark, who remark;

who first make the stains.

Keeping in mind that to paint (*peindre*) and to write (*piesiu*) might not just be related, but could well be indistinguishable: hence Socrates' suspicion of, his warning against, *chirography*, marks made by the hand (*kheiros*). For, what represents (*darstellung*) quite possibly also speaks for (*vertretung*), speaks over, speaks in the voice of another —

prosopopoeia.

*I can't sleep
till I devour you*

— Marilyn Manson

And thus, quite possibly consumes the other.

Thus, one can perhaps either see — catch a glimpse of — Ruben Pang or the painting; where the painting bears witness to the marks made by, left behind by, him, or where Ruben Pang testifies to the possibility of making, of leaving behind, such marks. But that looking at one entails a blindness to the other; where the existence of each is a reminder that the other remains veiled from one; where both Ruben Pang and his paintings are memoirs of our blindness to the other; where the other is always only, and always already, a matter of faith.

Where both Ruben Pang and the painting are both the limit and the condition of each other.

Where neither the painting nor Ruben Pang can exist with nor without each other — at least not in the moment of being seen.

And where, the only reason one can speak of both at the same time, in the same space, is that one is doing nothing other than attempting to read the *absolute muteness* of the painting alongside the *silence* of Ruben Pang, attempting to listen to the *echoes between two silences*.

Where, responding to — even writing on — the paintings, to Ruben Pang, is nothing other than an attempt to attend to the *silent language of Ruben Pang* resounding with the *absolute muteness of the paintings*; attempting to listen to the cacophony that is *a language of painting* itself;

               and where what rises
               — insurrects in being left behind —
               is nothing other than

a painted language.

Passacaglia 3 — Serious Ladder

The patriarch's dreams of fraternal escape
Leaves a line direct to resolution
Amounting to the complete installation of the body
To your cloud of imagined favours

Necessary furnaces heal and alter
The sated appetites of a whispered pitch
Dry mouths to the bells of suggestion
And gradations of the spherical realms

Seven sorrows to seven joys[3]
Lightly torched affections and quiet passes
Each a capitulation to raise sunken cities
Like so many tilled and squelching grounds

Rising and falling mercury indicates
The lengths that spirits will go to inhabit
These tightened plains of the dyer's screen
These chiseled frames to the lights of adoration

Lim Lee Ching

[3] cf: Ted Hughes

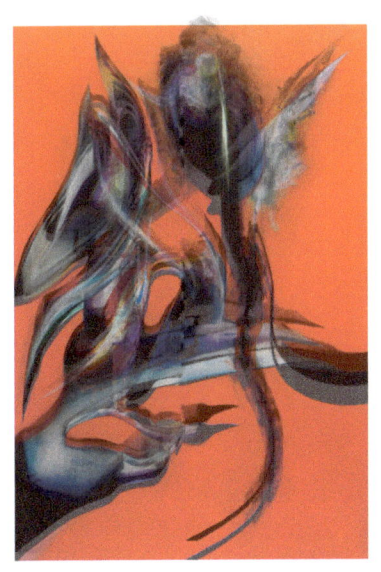
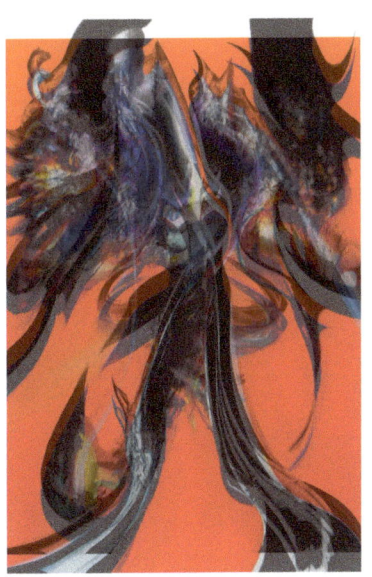
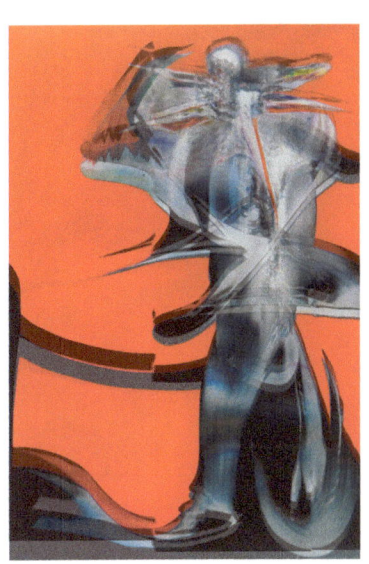

The Body
The Body

Contributors

Jeremy Fernando reads, and writes; and is the Jean Baudrillard Fellow at The European Graduate School. He works in the intersections of literature, philosophy, and the media; and his, more than twenty, books include *Reading Blindly*, *Living with Art*, *Writing Death*, and *in fidelity*. His writing has also been featured in magazines and journals such as *Arte al Límite*, *Berfrois*, *CTheory*, *Full Bleed*, *Qui Parle*, *TimeOut*, and *VICE*, amongst others; and has been translated into French, Italian, Japanese, Spanish, and Serbian. Exploring other media has led him to film, music, and the visual arts; and his work has been exhibited in Seoul, Vienna, Hong Kong, and Singapore. He is the general editor of the thematic magazine *One Imperative*; and is a Fellow of Tembusu College at The National University of Singapore.

Lim Lee Ching is the author of *Pure and Faultless Elation Emerging from Hiding*, a collection of poetry, as well as *The Works of Tomas Tranströmer: The Universality of Poetry*.

Ruben Pang works without a preconceived image of the final composition. His artistic practice evolves throughout the painting process, removing the boundary between abstraction and representation, and his vibrant and ethereal work combines fluid technique with a kaleidoscopic palette. This approach allows the imagery to surface spontaneously, which Pang describes as « visual syncopation, like searching for a melody in white noise ». Using oil paint and alkyd resin, Pang paints, scratches, and erases his paintings using brushes, hands, palette knives, and sandpaper, revealing layers of colour that reflect projections of his psyche. Pang works on aluminium panels, which allows him greater freedom to transform the image as it develops. His work explores medium and method, creating a feeling of dynamism while testing the boundaries of colour, form, and transparency.

His recent international shows include a solo exhibition, *The Glass Eye Opens* with Noosa Regional Gallery, *Aetheric Portraiture* with Primae Noctis Art Gallery in Lugano, Switzerland and a group exhibition, *Deep SEA* with Primo Marella Gallery in Milan, Italy. Locally, he has exhibited and performed in the Singapore Art Museum, Lasalle College of the Art's Praxis and Project Space, The Substation, and Chan Hampe Galleries. After graduating from the Lasalle College of the Arts in 2010 with a Diploma in Fine Art he received the Winston Oh Travelogue Award (2010), the Georgette Chen Arts Scholarship (2009-2010), the Lasalle Award for Academic Excellence, and was a finalist in the Sovereign Asian Art Prize in 2010 and 2011.

Sarah and Schooling is a two-woman graphic design studio based in Singapore. They connect ideas, visualise concepts, and develop design strategies that best communicate the needs and objectives of their clients. An ardent supporter of Singapore's literary scene, the studio is actively involved in designing books and publications across multiple genres. Their capabilities and experience stretch beyond publications, reaching other creative disciplines such as visual identity and branding, art directing, editorial design, web design, copywriting, and conducting workshops.

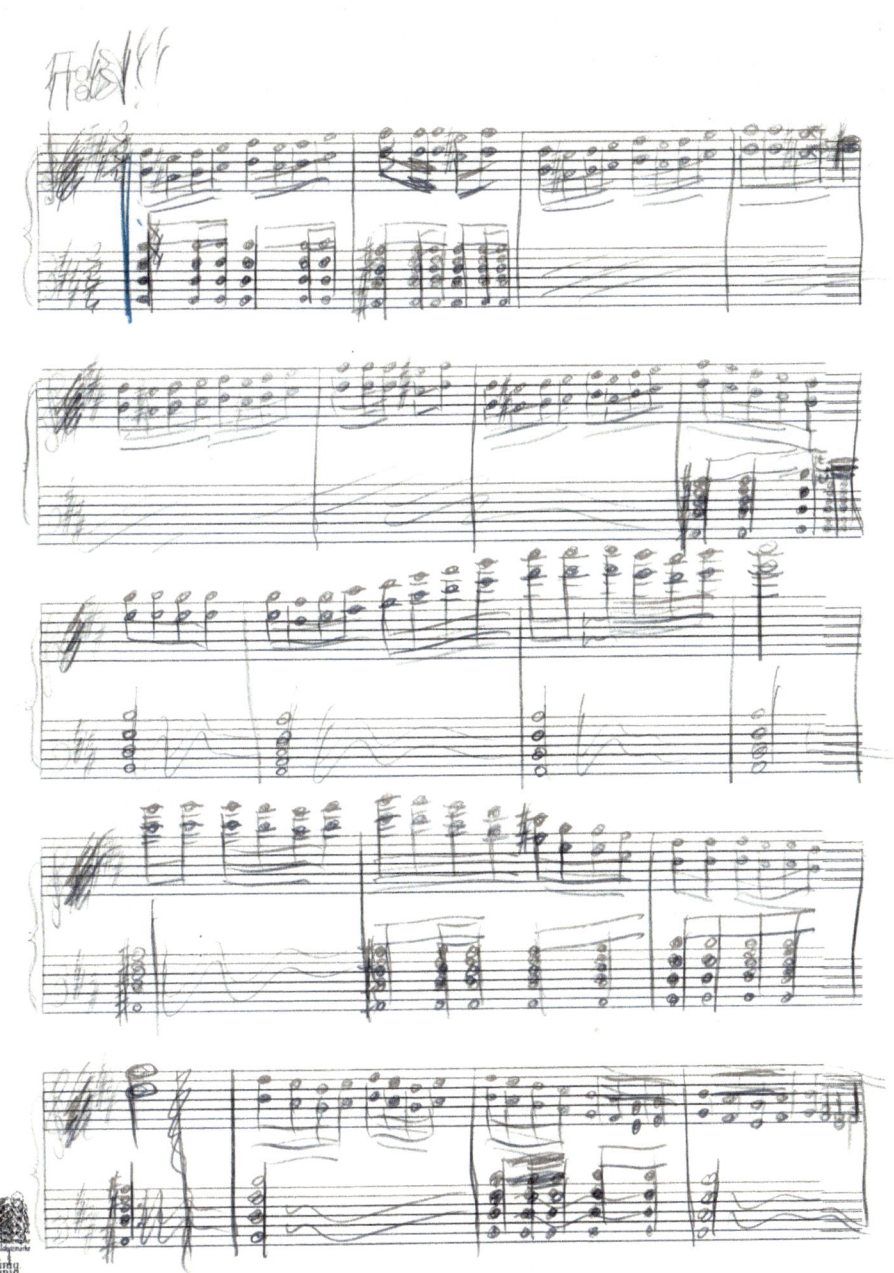

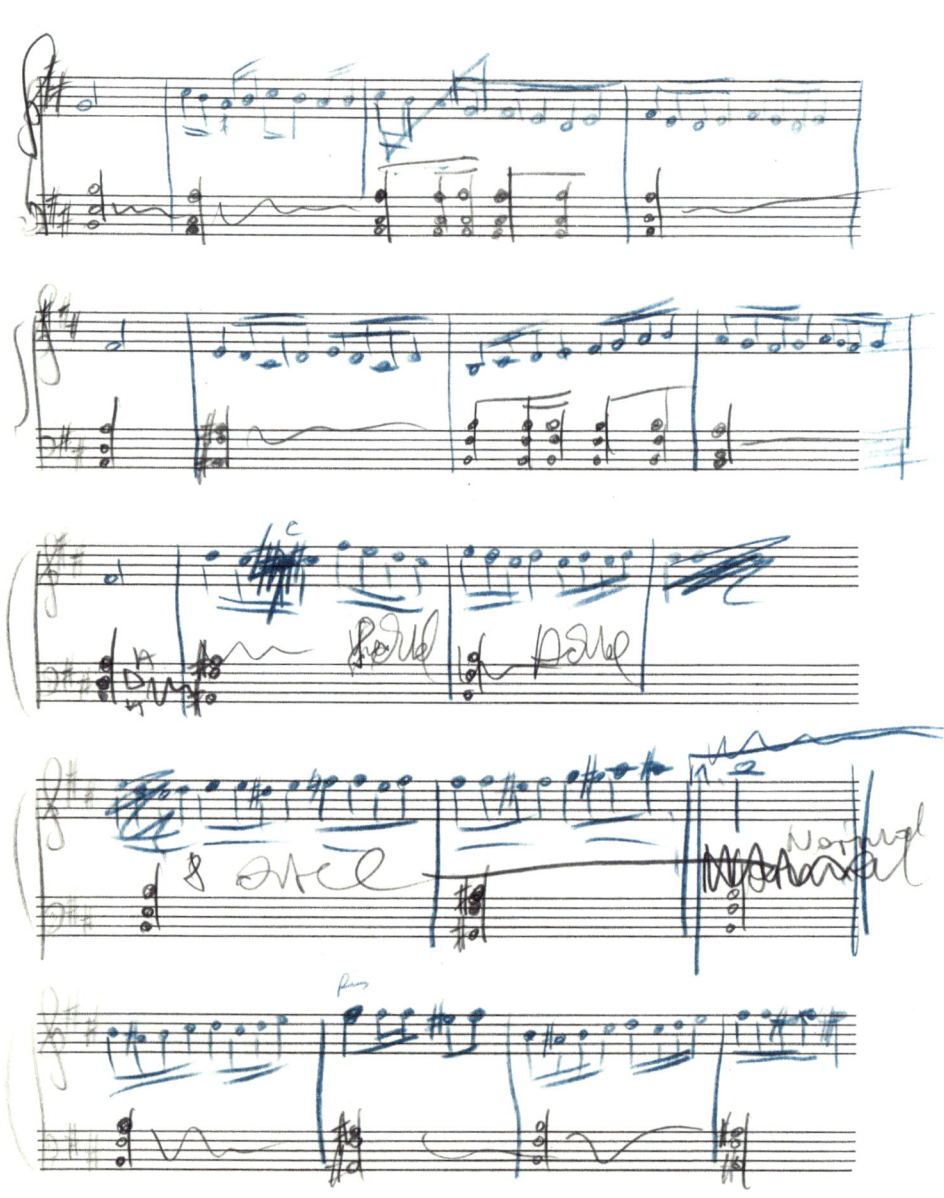